378.1   78404

BUCK

The master's wife

		DATE DUE	

The Master's Wife

The Master's Wife

POLLY STONE BUCK

ALGONQUIN BOOKS

of Chapel Hill

1989

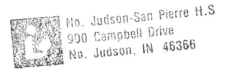

Published by
Algonquin Books of Chapel Hill
Post Office Box 2225
Chapel Hill, North Carolina 27515-2225
a division of
Workman Publishing Company, Inc.
708 Broadway
New York, New York 10003

Design by Barbara E. Williams

LIBRARY OF CONGRESS
CATALOGING-IN-PUBLICATION DATA

Buck, Polly Stone.
  The master's wife / by Polly Stone Buck.
    p. cm.
  ISBN 0-912697-92-X : $15.95
    1. Buck, Norman Sydney, 1892– . 2. College
teachers—United States—Biography. 3. Buck,
Polly Stone. 4. Teachers' wives—United States—
Biography. 5. Yale University—History. I. Title.
LD6331.B83B83 1989
378.1'2'092—dc20   89-15083
                                              CIP

FIRST EDITION

To the Fellows, staff, and students of Branford
during my husband's tenure as Master
and especially to the many Yale boys
who gave their blood in 1950
in an effort to save the life
of one of his little daughters

The Master's Wife

1

We were happily settled in an 1820 Connecticut farm-
house in the little country town of North Haven, just sixteen
miles from the college where my faculty husband earned our
daily bread, when suddenly the bombshell exploded that put
an end to our peaceful suburban life.

It happened on a late spring afternoon in 1942 when the
air was fragrant with apple blossoms, when snails and larks
were where Browning put them for all time on thorns and
wings respectively, and I was resting in the halcyon belief
that all was right with the world—at least, with our small
segment of it. If the bomb had gone off on a frigid December
day when the yard was glare ice and the driveway deep in
snow to be shoveled, the furnace out of kilter, and all of us
coughing and sniffling with three vaporizers running all
night, this chapter would probably never have been written,
for I should have advanced none of these demurrers, and
leaped at the chance of being rescued.

But it was spring, a spring afternoon out in the Connecticut countryside, and the lilacs were in bloom. When I
heard my husband's car drive up, I went out as usual to meet
him, and he immediately gave me the fatal news. The
master of Branford College (one of ten large residential halls

on the Yale campus that housed upperclassmen) had re-signed, and the university president had asked him—Steve, my husband, who was at the time dean of one thousand freshmen—to take over the post. As master of this beautiful old residence hall, he would be directly responsible for the welfare of three hundred or so Yale sophomores, juniors, and seniors who lived, dined, and competed in intramural sports together as residents of Branford.

While I was still gasping with delight over this well-deserved recognition and promotion, he added the rest of the information that wrecked the whole thing. With the job went required residence for the entire family in Branford's master's house, in a suite of rooms within the hall itself, and we were to move in immediately.

Move? Leave here? Immediately?

I burst into a torrent of tears. No, no, I wouldn't go; wild horses couldn't make me! This was *our home*, that we had made ourselves, where we had lived all of our married life! We had brought it back from a derelict wreck to a smiling, beautiful place—a visitor had once said it was the prettiest place on the road between New Haven and Boston. We had planned, and dug, and planted, and watched things grow—trees, shrubs, flowers. Our three babies—Prima, Secunda, and Tercia—had been brought home here from the hospital, grown from babies to little girls. It was a perfect home for them. Outdoors, there were climbable old apple trees, and a big grassy yard full of playground equipment; for rainy days, a long porch, a sloping-roofed attic, and a huge old barn. House and yard met all our desires; we loved every inch of both of them!

In childhood, neither my husband nor I had been allowed to own pets, and now for several years we had been the happy owners of a New Hampshire coon cat and a cocker spaniel, both beloved family members who reveled in country living. We were less than half an hour's drive from my husband's office and classroom. *Everything* combined to be a perfect setup, and we loved it so! Peace, beauty, happiness, our *home!* Created by our own hands, how could we be expected just to walk away from it all? Never, never! I wouldn't, and that was final.

To go from this into the grim heart of a city? How could he even consider it for a minute? No, no, a thousand times no! I babbled, I wept, I gnashed, I poured out protestations! To give up our two acres to be cramped in a city apartment— which was what a college master's house amounted to— with no yard for sunny days, or porch for rainy ones; where would our children play? How would our animals, used to running free, manage? Since the cat was country-bred and utterly unacquainted with traffic, I was sure eight-year-old Percy would fall under car wheels on his first day in a city.

And what about our dog, Nancy? I am not a "doggy woman." My idea of the utmost in dog exercising that should be required of a responsible adult possessing an immortal soul is to let the animal in and out when it thinks it is on the wrong side of a door. With other complications and duties in town, I certainly couldn't run around city sidewalks on the end of a dog's leash, even if I wanted to, which I didn't. And, could we simply walk off and leave our magnificent vegetable garden, with a corner patch of sweet corn (eight minutes from stalk to buttered ears on the table!), an asparagus bed where we had planted the roots a foot deep to produce for fifty years? Could we bear to go away from the two pear trees outside the dining room windows that filled the view with white blossoms, the big black-limbed cherry ("loveliest of trees . . . hung with bloom along the bough"), and my flowers; oh, all my flowers! The lilac hedge, the climbing silver moon rose that I had layered myself, the huge white and pink peonies in the perennial border, the little shady wildflower garden, wrested from the woods and brought home by shovelfuls, the cutting garden, the little knot garden of fragrant herbs, the hot bed and cold frame in a protected angle of the barn for starting things— oh, I could not give up all these! They were my heart! I poured this all out in tearful, passionate protest.

It wasn't just the children and the pets and myself that would lose so much; when I thought what it would mean for *him*, I cried even harder. If his office were right in the house, as it would be in the city, there would be no excuse for his not working there every minute, early and late. Between teary gulps, I reminded him that now, once he turned into our driveway, his time was his own. And there were those dozens and dozens of interesting things that he so enjoyed doing around the house. It was really his clever hands that had made the house the pleasant place to live in that it was. How often had he fearlessly mounted a ladder to fix a leak in the roof, or touch up a bit of chipped chimney? To crouch and creep along under the eaves pouring insulating material into the walls and ceilings? He had pressed putty around rattling windowpanes, put in needed shelves everywhere, taken off the old house's ill-fitting doors and planed their bottoms. Many a time he had gotten a balky pump going again, laid out the broken furnace in pieces on the cellar floor, found the trouble, and reassembled it.

There was also the haven of the grand old barn, into which in inclement weather, or if he didn't fancy having his work looked over and commented on, he used to disappear for whole Saturday afternoons or Sundays, hammering and sawing to his heart's content. There were constant orders arriving from nursery catalogs to dig holes for—no one could dig such wonderful holes as he could! If idle hands spelled discontent, he had surely been the world's most contented man. He so loved tools and machinery, things that ran by motors, like leaf-rakers and snow-blowers. He always over-spent the amount in the budget labeled "hardware." I could not bear to think of his giving up these things he loved so well. If we were to live in town—for 80 High Street was in the heart of downtown New Haven, in a university-owned build-ing, too—he would have none of them. We would not even know whether the roof leaked or not, having about three floors above us; the university power plant furnished heat to all the buildings so there would never be the satisfaction of showing the furnace who was boss. There were sure to be already more shelves than we had things to put on them, and I was certain that the university had a whole army of grounds workers who would take over all his beloved outdoor chores.

They would be the ones who shifted the storm windows and screens at the proper seasons, *they* would cut the grass with mammoth mowers of fifteen-foot cutter-bars, and trim the edges—a garden refinement we had coveted here in the country, but never quite achieved. When the ground was white and the scrape of shovels and the roar of snowplows filled the air, it was they, not Steve, who, toasty-warm in woolens and anoraks, would shift the gears on those orange behemoths that men so adore (I have never understood why). There would be *absolutely nothing* for him to do either inside or outside.

Of course he would be far from being bored by the lack of things to do, but they would be such dull things! And so monotonous! Nothing but mountains of tiresome desk work and committees and interviews, and those insuperable personal problems that the hundreds of boys for whom he would be responsible always managed to come up with. There would be no more of the fascinating things he did now as lord of the manor.

I had poured out so many and such vehement arguments against this diabolical move that I had to pause for breath. And it was then, through my brimming tears, that I really saw for the first time my husband's radiant face, and realized that he was saying something, and to my utter amazement, this is what it was:

"Just think, Polly, what it will mean! Not only will I have one of the most interesting jobs in running a college, but look at the side benefits! No more lawn to mow, leaves to rake, snow to shovel, storm windows to be eternally shifting around, no pump or furnace to wrestle with, no highway traffic to fight morning and evening in all weathers!" He drew a deep breath. "It will be heaven!"

I was brought up short, and for the first time suddenly wondered whether he had been as entranced with the problems of house maintenance all these years as I had believed. Perhaps, yes, for him, I suppose it would be heaven, but I still was convinced that for the children and the animals and me, we were leaving heaven for the other place.

"I hated to come and tell you this," he said gently, "for I know how much this home means to you, and your life in town will be completely different. No yard for the children, no growing things for you. But I promise you, there will be many compensations, perhaps enough. But even if there were none, we must do it. Running this place with so little help has gotten too much for us. I need to give more time to my university work, and you haven't any life at all but that of a housekeeper and gardener. Just look at your hands! And when did you last touch the piano? The children will soon be ready for school, and that will mean driving them back and forth to town daily. We've had a wonderful life here, but frankly, it is killing us both. We've got to choose between whether I am to be a college administrator and teacher, or a house maintenance man, and whether you are to be a lady or a drudge. Polly, my very dear, will you come with me and help me run one of the colleges?"

So there it was, laid on the line. Of course I mopped up my tears and even managed a lopsided grin of sorts as I said that certainly I would go. We would all go, adjust to what we found there, and plunge into a new sort of living. Although he put it like a question, the villain had already accepted the appointment even before he told me anything about it! My wanting desperately not to go cut no ice whatever. It was already a *fait accompli*.

That night, I lay awake a long time thinking it all over, and coming to the conclusion that I had been too precipitate in agreeing to move. I was not at all sure that we could maneuver gracefully as a family in such an exposed part of civilization, right in the center of the university; our scheme of living had been laid out on carefree country proportions. I had said I would go, but as the dark hours ticked along, I kept thinking up reasons not to.

When morning came, I set about explaining to my husband all over again why we simply *couldn't*, and that was all there was to it. To my surprise, he then told me that instead of saying "aye, aye, sir" immediately, as I had inferred, when the proposition had been put to him he had thought of all these objections of mine and presented them to the university. But they needed and wanted him for the job, and were willing to go to a good deal of trouble to get him. Protests were listened to; objections ironed out. Just name what changes we wanted made, and they would be started on immediately. So he did, and they were. The powerful powers that be said abracadabra, or some such formula, and things had already begun to happen.

A few of our problems they were powerless to change. They would have been insoluble to the angel Gabriel himself; providing other children, for instance, as playmates for ours. The colleges were situated in the business part of New Haven where there were no other homes but the masters' houses. These were perfect for a couple of adults, or if the children were old enough to be away at boarding school or college, which was often the case, for masters were chosen usually in their fifties or forties, and their children, if any, had had time to reach their teens. Rarely were there any youngsters living in masters' houses, and at the present time, all other masters' houses were sadly childless. We had to face it. Our three-, four-, and seven-year-old daughters would have only each other for companionship.

Some time later, our youngest daughter was to write succinctly about the plight of her and her sisters in these early years at Branford: "I was borne in North Haven my father was made master of Brandford collage so we moved to

8

the masters house. My two sisters who were older than me were given the best rooms I was left the other. The pepole next door were called Smith they have three children but they are no good to us for they are groan."

There would also definitely be no yard just outside the house in which the three of them might play. There was a yard; there were, in fact, four perfectly beautiful courtyards, but they were showplaces, and not for children's games. The trees were not climbable ones; they had no horizontal limbs from which a child's swing could be hung where little feet could wear a hardbitten oval of bare earth underneath.

But the university recognized that these three children existed, that, you might say, we were stuck with them and were silly enough to have become over the years quite fond of all three. We could not be expected now to drown them, or put them up for adoption; we had to bring them along, and the university knew as well as we did that young high spirits cannot be completely suppressed. So they benevolently would make provision for these impedimenta, although it could not be in the Quadrangle courts, conveniently just beneath our windows, and within calling distance of my voice. Three long and traffic-filled blocks away, behind Alumni Hall, there was a vacant bit of university-owned property on which grew a large horse chestnut tree; this they offered to turn over to us as a playground for our children. All their play equipment would be brought in from the country and put there. The swing uprights, which only a few weeks before Steve had spent an entire Saturday afternoon sinking in concrete (to last for our grandchildren), would be wrenched from the earth by university groundsmen and reset here, as well as the sandbox, with a new load of grim, grey

Connecticut shore sand, and "under the spreading (horse) chestnut tree," joyful shrieks and screams would be permitted without the penalty of jail or instant death. With relief, they checked the children off the list of objections.

Next came the question of how to arrange for the dog and cat, whom we had had even longer than we had had the children. We had no intention of pitching them out of the car on a country road to fare as best they could, or turning them over to an animal shelter to be put to sleep if not adopted within two weeks.

The eight-year-old cat, Percy, free-roaming Nimrod of the surrounding fields, scourge of baby rabbits and field mice (and I regret to say, also sometimes of unwary birds), would, alas, have to be an in-house dweller. I didn't know at the time that that was not such a terrible sentence, that many cats live long and happily indoors, and that his previous days outside had simply been fun for him, and not a requisite for life itself. I knew cats did not have to be walked for exercise, but I thought that any breathing animal should have fresh air every day. Instead of telling me that I was crazy (which they should have done), the university considerately worked out a plan for one of their carpenters to build a three-by-three-by-sixteen-foot wire cage in the dry moat outside of a basement door, and hidden from the sidewalk traffic by a stone wall. Here pampered Percy was to do his deep breathing every day. (I don't know what they thought of *me* for suggesting such a thing.) A little walled corner of one of the courts was also discovered to which the dog could be taken, to be called henceforth "Nancy's yard."

Children and livestock were thus provided for, but there remained *me*. Without a garden and a place to dig in the earth and watch what I could bring forth from it, I did not think I could survive. But Steve had not forgotten the Little Woman in his bargaining. Since the university had never before had to deal with a master's wife whose passion was digging in the dirt and making things grow, it was a dilemma, for not only was there not a square foot of diggable dirt available at this new home, but even a window box could not be allowed to spoil its appearance.

Yet to them, as to Disraeli, all problems were solvable, the impossible only took a little longer. At the top of Hill-house Avenue, they had just acquired, through the will of a New Haven citizen, the Hillhouse Mansion, which had a large fenced-in vegetable garden. Several of the university officers—the president, treasurer, and chaplain, among others—who had no kitchen gardens at their homes, had been assigned plots in it, and one was now to be given to me. Two more keys would be added to my already heavy key-chain, one to the garden gate and the other to a roomy toolhouse which we gardeners were to share inside the enclosure.

My husband's own new requirements were easy. He already had offices, secretaries, and student office aides, and would now need only more of them. They were there for the assigning. There was no quibble from him over what he was giving up in the country; he was delighted to relinquish it. His individual cup was brimming and running over.

"Now," said Yale, leaning back in its official chair, having taken care of objections raised about wife, children, and pets, "Let's have no more nonsense!"

And there was no more. I knew when I was licked. Any other details could be worked out as they arose, once we were in residence and a routine established. I gave in, permanently, meekly, and more or less gracefully.

I had known all the time that I should have to. Even if by some possibility the decision to go could have been made by a family show of hands and paws, I should have lost. Percy, remembering baby rabbits and his jungle ancestors, might have voted with me, but no one else would have. Nancy would not have cast a vote yea or nay, for she didn't give a continental where she lived, as long as her adored master came home every night. A cold-water walk-up flat in Bridgeport would have been all right with her, provided Steve was there. And the little daughters, archtraitors, were overjoyed at the prospect of exchanging the silence of the country for a place where fire engines, streetcars, ambulances, and Good Humor wagons made life worth living.

AS TIME went on, I would come to love devotedly this Branford College to which I came kicking and screaming. When one June day, several years later, I reminded Steve wistfully in our flowerless home on High Street, how on an afternoon out in the country I had cut forty peonies for the house and to distribute to friends, he countered with, "Would you swap boys for peonies?" and the passionate answer was *"Never!"*

We listed our precious, forsaken home with a real estate agency that rented it for a couple of years, then sold it.

For the next seventeen years, we were the residents of the Branford master's house.

2

*B*ranford College occupies half of a great stone quadrangle covering almost the entire block between York, Elm, and High streets in New Haven, and construction on it was begun just before World War I. At one corner, a crown tower with a carillon of bells rises high above all the surrounding buildings, and is the Yale landmark, visible for miles around. Only dry moats and low stone walls separate the quadrangle from the sidewalks of the city streets, and at first glance, it seemed to be a grim, forbidding fortress, but inside the great iron gates are charming secluded courtyards of cobblestones or green lawns which no grass-killing footsteps or games are ever allowed to desecrate. They are planted with elms and maples, smaller flowering trees, clumps and hedges of yew. Ropes of wisteria frame the windows, pendent fountains of forsythia fall down the walls, and in season there are banks of spring bulbs—snowdrops, tulips, and daffodils "that come before the swallow dares, and take the winds of March with beauty." Along the walks, there are occasional benches made of stone or the teakwood masts of former British warships. It has often been called the most beautiful college building in America, and it lacks only the patina of age to rival Oxford.

Originally planned to house the senior class, when Yale adopted "the college plan" in 1935, this building was transformed into two of the new colleges, Saybrook and Branford, and sophomores and juniors were allowed to join seniors as occupants. The one called Branford was now to be our home. There were living and dining quarters there for several hundred students, suites for a few bachelor Fellows, and three floors of the building taking up one side of the main courtyard was a spacious apartment for the family of the master of the college.

I had already been in the master's house several times as a guest, at cocktail parties for Fellows and their wives, receptions on Parents' Day, and even a formal dinner or so for important university guests, but now that it was decided that we were to move into it, Steve met me there at 80 High Street one day to go over the place room by room with a thirty-foot tape measure to help us figure out where to place our furniture.

I had to admit that it was a lovely place, for while on one side only four stone steps separated its front door from the noisy, busy High Street, on the other, overlooking the court, there was unbelievable beauty, peace, and quiet.

The house's interior was charming, with diamond-paned casement windows stretching along an entire wall in each room both upstairs and down. The living room was quite long, with a fireplace at each end, and its windows looked out onto the most beautiful of the four courts. The formal dining room was also a long room, with such a handsome table that I immediately decided that meals here were verboten for our children as long as they were at the stage of spilling apple sauce and Jell-o and turning over milk glasses. (Fortunately, one of the stops in the path of the electric dumbwaiter from the kitchen was in the upstairs hall just outside the door of what we planned for their play room, and their tray meals could be sent up on this.)

Since the university often called in the aid of the master's house to entertain its guests, the first floor had been furnished under the eye of a professional decorator, often with antiques, and paintings that the university art gallery did not have space to hang. The decorator had also been responsible for a suite of rooms on the third floor for special university guests assigned to Branford, but on the second floor the master's family had a free hand. We could take down our back hair and relax comfortably on our own sofas and chairs, shredded by the cat's claws, and the rugs that had suffered their bit during the cocker's puppyhood.

The second floor bedrooms were strung out in a line on both sides of a long hall, giving them either a view over the lovely inside courtyard, or across High Street to the elm-studded Old Campus, criss-crossed with walks, with its two college chapels and the buildings where the freshmen lived. At one end of this hall were the guest rooms, then a master bedroom, and four other bedrooms for the family. Everywhere were spacious closets, and enough shelves and cupboards to store or display family belongings. A large room, which the former master and his wife had used for an upstairs sitting room, we would turn over to the children for their playroom. It was lined with bookshelves and cupboards for toys and games, and there was adequate space for the three doll houses, the work table on which they would have their meals, a day bed, and plenty of space left for what the children called "monkeying around." (Later, one of the students leaving for the war gave the children his upright piano, and it found a home in this room, too.)

Since live-in servants in a house this size were customary when the plans were drawn, at the end of the hall were two bedrooms and a white-tiled bath for servants, and a back stairway that went down into the kitchen.

And here, after the somewhat down-at-heel kitchen in our former home, the kitchen quarters simply took my breath away: three rooms, all with floors of arresting black and white linoleum squares, and walls of glass-fronted dish cupboards. Down the center of one of the rooms stretched a stainless steel work table. (One day, after we had settled in, I was showing one of the freshman counsellor medical students over the house, and when we came to this, he cried out in delight, "A perfect operating table! Bring down all the children, Mrs. B., and I'll take their tonsils out for nothing!")

There were two large refrigerators, an ample plate-warming oven, an electric stove that put my wood-burning range in the country to shame. Electric dishwashers were unknown as yet; a pair of stainless steel sinks which were at that time the last word in kitchen plumbing was placed under a battery of windows that looked into the large courtyard, so that while she was working, the human dishwasher had a view fit for an art calendar.

I decided on the spot that if I ever lost my job as the master's wife, I should apply for that of his cook.

And there was still another floor—the basement. Here was the laundry, to which we would bring our new Bendix washing machine, of which we were very proud. These were still such novelities that householders often drew up their chairs in front and watched in fascination its round glass window where the clothes were tumbling around. Electric clothes dryers had not yet come in but the Branford laundry room boasted four six-foot drying racks with gas burners underneath. (Only a short time after we moved in to 80 High Street, freezers, automatic dishwashers and clothes dryers became available, and were installed.) There was also in the basement a game room for the ping-pong table, and storage rooms to delight any householder's heart: a wood room—for there were five fireplaces in the house, a pantry for reserve canned goods, and with racks where wine bottles could recline comfortably on their sides; a storage space for furniture not needed at the moment, but might be again (such as the cribs, playpen, and potty chairs); and a box room. This last was a great joy to me. How wonderful never to have to throw away a clean, beautiful box, but have a whole basement room in which to store it against the problematical future day when one of just that size might be needed!

The basement was also the home of an incinerator, where daily the building's janitor burned the master's house trash, which included not only the wastepaper basket contents but kitchen refuse—coffee grounds, egg shells, fruit and vegetable peelings, etc. That estimable man would also carry away to some unknown destination—I was not to know or be concerned with where—our empty cans, bottles, and so on. This meant that there would be no more trips, as formerly, in a loaded station wagon to the town dump. These rides to "de dump" had been a delight to the children, who always roamed around looking for treasures during the unloading process, and sometimes even Steve, when he was chauffeur, would come back with a retrieved piece of pipe or board that was "just the size he needed." But I personally could give up dump trips with relief!

On completion of our tour of the house, Steve produced from his pocket and turned over to me a great bunch of keys. "These are for you," he said. "Guard them with your life. It is essential that *everything* be kept locked *all the time.*"

After our free and easy life in the suburbs, these keys rather overwhelmed me. There were keys to the front door, to service and garage doors, all of which opened on High Street; cellar keys to a storage pantry, wine closet, laundry, wood room, game room, box room. There was a key to the door giving onto the front moat; first floor keys of garage to kitchen, office outside door to the court, and another from our front hall to the office—all making a full and very heavy keyring. There was also a master key, that said so in boldly imprinted letters—MASTER BRANFORD—which if lost and picked up by the wrong party would let him into any and all doors, even those to students' rooms. I was so absolutely terrified at the thought of losing this one that I refused to carry it, and preferred, to the responsibility of carrying around such a blatantly proclaimed open-sesame to every corner of the building, being loaded down like a prison warden with all the individual keys. And there were four more: the two car keys, and two to the Hillhouse garden and tool house, which had already been given me and that I now put with the others. For the first time, I understood the "key basket" which housekeepers in Victorian novels always carried, and how goody-goody Esther Summerson in *Bleak House* could write at the end of practically every chapter that she "gave her basket of housekeeping keys such a shake that they sounded like little bells."

Although undeniably beautiful, it was apparently a prison into which we were moving, and I was to be one of the chief wardens.

3

Once the decision had been made to leave our eminently liveable home in the suburbs for this hands-off castle, I determined to believe that it was, as my husband had said, all for the best, with enough compensations for what we were giving up. Weep no more, my lady, I told myself, for overwhelming advantages are now to be heaped on our heads, and I must concentrate on them, and forget things like the asparagus bed. We have been saved, in spite of ourselves, from the disastrous results of our short-sighted family planning, for of all fallacies, the most fallacious and absurd is that the best place to raise children is in the country, close to nature. The country is instead the worst possible place for children, and for the harried parents of them. Children don't give a fig for nature; they much prefer the tinkle of a Good Humor truck bell.

We did not realize this, of course, at the time when we were breaking our necks to find a country house, and rapturously slaving to make it what we thought was a perfect home for them. Children need other children much more than they do daisies and sunsets. Even healthy and well children are from birth onward constantly having to be hauled to a doctor for shots or one thing or another, and later to a dentist.

If we were still in the country when they were ready for school, this would mean someone's constant driving back and forth (for "someone," read "mother"), whereas in town, there might easily be a school within walking or certainly bus distance, and there would probably be a Sunday school, too. On Monday afternoons, there were Miss Darling's dancing classes, where generations of faculty children had learned to waltz and polka, while a rank of complacent mothers sat around the perimeter of the Lawn Club ballroom and watched. The children could learn to swim in a supervised, filtered pool at the Y, instead of in a muddy pond up the road, alive with blood suckers; to ice skate in the city arena the year around, instead of on this same little pond, and that only a few days out of the whole winter, on ice that might or might not hold over several feet of black water. Best of all, they would be constantly associating with adults, and would learn to talk easily with them, or more important, to listen. In no time at all they would develop into charming, intelligent children, instead of the present round-eyed little oafs who hid bashfully behind the safety of Mummy's skirts or took to their heels when the occasional daytime visitor came to the country house.

There were even some advantages for me—quite a lot of them, when I came to list them honestly, although giving up my flowers and my yard was at the moment tearing my heart out. Instead of being a horny-handed gardener and a chauffeur delivering and collecting for the multiple engagements and classes that the different ages of our brood soon would inevitably demand, I could in town lead a pleasant adult life of my own. I would put lotion on my hands every night—which I was usually too tired to do before—even though they wouldn't need it as much; nothing dries hands like digging in a garden. With both the university library and the city library nearby, I might even occasionally read a book. And we were to be within walking distance of the many cultural things that Yale and New Haven had to offer. Yes, everything was surely for the best in this best of all possible worlds. With heart now high (most of the time), and sleeves rolled up, all of the time, the actual packing began.

July of that year in Connecticut was a sizzler, and it was during that month that we moved in town. The garden came in with a bang, and I gathered bounteous vegetables for our daily meals and thriftily canned everything that we couldn't eat on the spot. String beans—ye gods, how fast they grow! I can easily believe that Jack's beanstalk reached the sky. When I finished at one end of a row, and straightened my weary back, I saw with horror that the beans at the other end had matured in the meantime and were ready to be picked.

Every day, in between stints in the garden and standing over a hot range with glass jars bubbling like mad in a preserving kettle, I cleared out closets and bookcases and dish shelves, and packed the contents in brown cardboard liquor boxes or garden bushel baskets—each one loaded with just a little more than I could lift, but which I *did* lift and then stowed in the station wagon backed up to the side door. Late in the afternoon, I tidied up my by-that-time-very-untidy self and the three little girls, who were even untidier (for they had in the meantime been having a de-lightful, unsupervised day of playing in as much mud as their combined efforts could manufacture with a waterpot and a sandbox). Together we drove to our new house and unloaded.

College classes were running the year-round that year, so the place was alive with students. Branford boys were angels about offering to heave heavy boxes and baskets inside for me. I suppose they were interested in seeing what the big and little females looked like who were moving into their stronghold.

After a week or so of this, when I had carried in all the small things I could pack and manage myself, the final day came.

> The coach is at the door at last,
> Goodbye, goodbye to everything!

Farewell to the two old pear trees by the dining room windows—lovely beyond words in the spring—and to the lilac hedge around the curving driveway! Farewell to the copper beech, with its robin nest, to all the old apple trees! Cohen and Powell's enormous truck, itself as big as a house, took the station wagon's place at the side door, and a procession of chairs, sofas, tables, and beds was snatched from under us and disappeared into its giant maw. The grand piano was lifted ignominiously off its legs and stood up sideways with the other furniture.

My husband superintended getting the things off from the North Haven house, and I was stationed in town as receiver of goods. We had carefully measured and figured out just where everything was to go, Steve had printed room directions on stringed tags, and the children had tied these to everything. They proved to be utterly useless, for he had written on them things like "north-east bedroom." He actually thought of the rooms that way, but the moving men had no more idea than a jack rabbit of how the house lay in regard to the compass, nor had I. In order to get my compass bearings, I have to have a sun either rising or setting, and neither of these things happened during the midday hours of our move. But I knew where each piece was supposed to go, so eventually everything wound up in its correct place, and Steve congratulated himself that his tags had been of inspired efficiency.

The piano was put back together, chairs and tables scattered around here and there, mattresses crashed onto bedsteads, and beds made up from the linens that I had brought in days before and that were already at home on the shelves in an upstairs linen closet.

The now-empty truck roared away, with the movers hanging their legs off the tailgate, waving to the little girls, and swigging down the cans of beer that Steve had thought to have in the icebox for them.

We were "in business, at the new location."

The leftovers from last night's dinner in the old house were produced and set out on the kitchen table, dog and cat food cans opened, and, weary almost unto death, we sat down to our first meal in the Branford master's house.

THE NEXT morning we awoke in our familiar beds to find a friendly sun slanting through the enchanting little diamond-paned windows, and with our well-known furniture there to hold out its arms to us and say, "Look! We are all here too! Welcome home!" The place to which I had so vigorously protested coming didn't seem too unfriendly or strange. Perhaps, as the days passed, we could work things out. Changes from time to time are inevitable for everyone; why should we be exempt?

I resolved to see to it that we held fast to all the old traditions and customs that we had known in our North Haven home, that the children would still know and care about country things, growing things, flowers, and birds. There *had* to be other birds around High besides English sparrows and pigeons, the only ones I had seen so far. The top of Harkness Tower was open, and the pigeons that swooped around the Green had made a regular dovecote of it. The former master here had told me that some of them got into the chimney of his office, and cooed and cooed and cooed until they almost drove him distracted. In desperation he sent for one of the maintenance men and told him that they had to cover the chimneys and keep those pigeons out.

"But they *are* covered," the man protested. "Every single one has a wire netting across the top; pigeons can't possibly get in."

"They are in this chimney!" stormed the master, "and I want them out!"

"There are no pigeons in this or any other chimney," the man stormed back.

At that moment there was a soft, scuffling sound, and a pigeon walked out of the fireplace.

We could not expect to have wildlife in the middle of a city, but there were a number of sassy little squirrels in the court, leaping from limb to limb, tree to tree, and even making stairways of the ivy and wisteria on the building walls, and staring in at us through upstairs windows. A boy

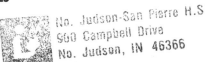

who lived on the floor above us swore that one made off from his room with an unopened can of mixed nuts.

"How did he know they were nuts?" I asked skeptically. "Don't tell me you think Yale squirrels can read labels."

He stuck to his story. "He must have looked at the picture on the can."

We would make do with squirrels and sparrows and pigeons through the winter if we must, but in spring we should expect something else. The annual offer of five cents to the child who saw the first robin would still be open.

"*Ten* cents," demanded the winner, by then a sophisticated four-year-old, that spring. "Things are higher in town."

One chapter of our lives had closed, that was all, but another had opened. Before it was over, both our dear pets Nancy and Percy would have died of old age and been buried in Nancy's little walled garden under the kitchen windows. (The university doesn't know it, for I didn't dare put up markers for either little grave.) The tiny daughters we brought along when we came would have become long-legged, strong-minded graduates of Wellesley and Mt. Holyoke, with Yale husbands.

What a chapter it turned out to be!

4

*F*or better or for worse, we were now installed in this lovely and spacious apartment which we were henceforth to call home, and adjustments began. Steve had told me beforehand that there would be compensations in our new life— "perhaps enough," he had said—and I believe there were. Most of the annoying things about living at Branford were either overbalanced by another convenience, or had redeeming features of their own.

Certainly one convenience, for Steve, was that of having his office in the same building in which we lived. The only offices attached to houses that I had seen before belonged to doctors and dentists. A sign out in front would say, "Please use side door for doctor's office," and I used to think how dreadful it must be for the family to have the groans and screams of patients floating into the house. But students are not patients, and don't generally groan and scream and get blood all over things during an office call. And students were not the only ones who sought out the master to solve their problems. I sometimes found it very convenient to ask his help too. Perhaps my dilemmas were not as momentous as those of Yale upperclassmen, but they seemed so to me at the time, for they were holding me up, and I couldn't get on with what I was doing until they were out of the way. Take a simple thing like opening a jar of pickles or applesauce for the children's supper. I often struggled to do it myself, but in vain. Formerly, with sixteen miles stretching between us, I couldn't call on him, of course, but now, with his office only two steps away, I could. I am not sure he was very happy over it, but I was in and out in less than a wink, not much of an interruption. One quick grasp of his strong hand was all it took.

And there was reciprocity, too, for if he sometimes found he had twenty minutes before an appointment in the middle of a weary afternoon, he could slip upstairs and take a quiet nap, confident that I would call him in time.

Another mistaken idea I formerly had of an office in the house was what an annoyance it must be to have one's husband constantly around, popping in at any inconvenient minute—such as when you were washing your hair—and always expecting a hot lunch. Someone said that the marriage service should include a vow on the man's part that he would not come home for lunch. I had never had to worry about this, for our home in the suburbs, while inconveniently too far for getting jars opened, was also too far to come for lunch. In town I learned that the lunch hour was the time for faculty committee meetings and confabulations. Bless their hearts, they had them in the college dining halls and men's clubs, and didn't bother their wives. Every bite they took went down with a report, a plan, a suggestion. No wonder so many of them had ulcers.

Another of the joys of living in town was being near things. Just across the Green from us were the theatres, movies, banks, and, best of all for me and a great help in my daily affairs, the stores. Before, when something gave out, or was needed, I put it on "the list," and sometimes had to wait a fortnight before I could get in town to shop for it. By that time, the list was so long that frequently I didn't get more than half of it attended to on that trip, but now, if I ran out of a certain shade of thread, for example, or needed some stiff muslin for a lining, I could trot down to Grossman's for it and be back in fifteen minutes. A Woolworth store was just as near, as was also a good hardware store, and beyond words was the convenience of having Yale station post office right across the street. No one ever lives near a post office, but now I did! At Christmas time, mailing packages was a piece of cake—I did them one or two at a time as I got them wrapped, and not waiting until a dozen were ready and I could barely stagger to the car with the load. No driving was involved now, either; I could just nip across the street.

Yes, there were many compensations. Perhaps the greatest one was that we began having an adult evening life again, going out to dinner with friends and to 8:30 P.M. things, like plays at the Shubert, and having season tickets for Woolsey and Sprague Hall concerts, only two blocks away. After a winter evening's concert, Steve and I could be asleep in bed while the rest of the audience was still bumbling around in the cold, trying to remember where they had parked the car.

We were never shackled to the house for lack of a baby-sitter, for high on the list of the benefits to be derived from living in town I would place the abundance and proximity of evening babysitters. Our children were in bed and out of the way by eight, were all sound sleepers, and our babysitting never entailed anything more arduous than taking any phone messages and being there if the house caught fire.

Almost any one of the college's three hundred boys would rather have studied alone in our living room (with permission to raid the cookie jar and icebox thrown in), than in his own room with several roommates. And when we got home, Steve was spared the usual nuisance of driving the sitter home half across town, which is where sitters invariably live.

The availability of the college dining hall was a great convenience, and we always took Sunday dinner there. If unexpected company swooped in on us at mealtime, as they often did, and the cupboard was bare of company food or a cook nonexistent (both of which often happened), it was a positive godsend simply to walk the guests across the court and have a much better dinner than I usually gave my family. People were always interested in seeing the beautiful dining hall, and sampling student menus.

The Hillhouse garden plot was a joy, in spite of its drawback of being at least a mile away from the house. I couldn't pop outside and do a bit of weeding whenever I had a little free time, or dash out at the last minute and cut flowers for the dinner table, or pick a tomato for my lunch sandwich; any trip had to be a planned, organized expedition, either taking the children along or making provision for someone to be at home with them. Both the garden and I suffered as a consequence, but it was a secure place, because firmly locked up all the time, where I raised tomatoes and peas, and chrysanthemums in the fall. The former Hillhouse family gardener had trained two rambler roses on the fence, and they furnished both our house and the altar in the little chapel in the Harkness Tower with June flowers.

Within the house itself, there were many things that made life easier. While the laundry was a completely day-lightless room in the basement, and I was apt to think with longing of how the clothes used to flap and dance in the breezes of the sunny backyard in our previous incarnation, I tried to concentrate instead on Branford's four purring, dependable little gas dryers, and remember the rainy days in the country, with needed wet things hanging forlornly around on long lines in the unheated shed, refusing to dry.

How had I ever lived without an electric dumbwaiter? Not only the children's meals but dozens of other things went up and down and spared our backs: wood for the fireplaces came up from the basement wood room, canned goods from the storage pantry. On Mondays the soiled clothes rode down, and after ministrations by the Bendix and the gas dryers, came triumphantly back to the second floor. Just the weekly stack of sheets alone would have been a heavy load to carry by hand both ways.

Through an opening in the kitchen wall to the incinerator just below, I could empty wastepaper baskets at any time. I did not have to wait for a day of absolute calm, and then find myself standing on a suddenly windy hill—for a brisk breeze always springs up the minute a match is lit—terrified that a falling ash would set all of North Haven in a blaze. There was no danger of fire here; everything was made of stone or steel. The basements, which ran under the whole block of buildings, were separated with great metal fire doors so heavy that when I passed through every day to put the cat in the moat, I had to hurl myself against them with all my weight to push them open. Any part of the building in which a fire might start could be completely cut off from any other, and any fire thus burn itself out.

They told me that this happened once. There were a

great many fancy bull's-eye windowpanes scattered around here and there in the leaded casements, several in every room, and during the spring holidays when the boys were gone, one of them, evidently put in the wrong way around, acted as a burning glass and set some papers on fire. From that it must have leaped to the curtains, and so merrily on. When the boys came back at vacation's end and opened their door, imagine their surprise to find the entire contents of their room burned to ashes, including the piano. Nothing outside the room was even smoked. (The story goes that there was one thing in the room that didn't burn: some fireplace wood bought from the student wood agency. It was too green to burn.)

If the children were not allowed to play on the court grass, at least the university cut it, and not Steve, with me crawling along on my hands and knees behind him, for seemingly mile after mile, trimming the edges with clippers.

And for at least three months of the winter, I sent up a constant prayer of gratitude for the university snow shovelers. When the roar and bump and scrape of snowplows and shovels filled the air, it was they, not we, who were doing it. To go to bed at night while the flakes were coming down, to wake in the night to find it still snowing, was now only to snuggle down under the blankets and think of how beautiful the whole white world would be in the morning, not to groan over what we had to do before the car could be gotten out. The car snuggled down gratefully too, for often it didn't have to come out into an icy world for weeks at a time. Those blessed groundsmen, cutters of grass, rakers of leaves, shovellers of snow!

We did, however, encounter a winter hazard that is

lacking in private homes, for an open window at Branford was an irresistible target for snowballs. Anyone who opened a window in a bedroom on a snowy night was pretty sure to have a few tossed in by passing students.

And for Steve, the sixteen-mile drive to work and back was now mercifully a thing of the past. On icy or foggy evenings out in the country, when my husband was in town for meetings, I used to stand at the window, fearful and anxious, watching the cars out on the turnpike creep by in the dangerous dimness, dreading to hear the telephone ring with news of an accident. Now a foggy evening only meant for me the unearthly beauty of the Harkness Tower and black elm branches disappearing up into the mist.

We missed the great orange full moons rising ponderously into our world from the flat fields that had lain across the road from us. Because of the many buildings hemming us in now, we never saw the moon until it was high in the sky and had lost its color, but it was even more magnificent when the view of it included Harkness crown tower and long tree shadows across the court.

> Behind the tower, the moon is rising now,
> Its light pours softly through each elm tree bough.
> And magic falls
> on Branford courts and walls,
> And we who love this place, now feel its spell.
> When day is done, and dusk and darkness come,
> How bright the lights shine out from every room!
> Row after row,
> The leaded casements glow,
> And for three years, these are the lights of home.

5

*F*or my husband, most things worked out more or less satisfactorily. The change had not been too much of a jolt for him; he was largely continuing to do things he had done before, only more so—much, much more so—but he had more office help with which to accomplish it. And he was doing his job in the same milieu; he had even lived as a bachelor Fellow for several years in one of the suites of this same building, so he felt quite at home. The main physical change for him was that he now had no sixteen-mile drive to take twice a day, for the office where he presided as dean of the freshmen was just across the street, and his Branford master's office opened off the house front hall. Being thus available for Yale's problems both day and night, he could now, as I had predicted, put in more working hours, and there was no reason (except that the human frame can't take it) why he shouldn't work around the clock. As a matter of fact, he often did this in the Branford office, comfortable in a bathrobe and with a pot of coffee for companionship. Boys coming home from an evening in New York frequently saw his light on at 2:00 or 3:00 A.M., tapped on the window, and came in for a chat and a cuppa.

But the lives of the rest of us were far from the same. In

34

my own case, my new tour of duty brought many personal adjustments. I cannot put my finger on any one as the first I had to make, for they all—a dozen at least—seemed to come at me at once. Perhaps the first was an immediate realization of how thoroughly insignificant and unimportant I had become. (Perhaps this was good for me.) After she and her husband moved into the White House, Mrs. John Quincy Adams entitled her diary "The Diary of a Nobody," and my daily journal could easily have been headed that too. A master's wife can't fail to know that she is only that; the newspapers alone will tell her in so many words, or rather, in the absence of any words at all, for when her husband's appointment is announced, *she* simply isn't mentioned.

There will probably be two columns about the new master—even a picture—when and where he was born, parents, where educated, degrees, honors, affiliations, publications, etc., but the wife who is giving up her home and putting behind her the pursuits she would otherwise have chosen, to share his life and responsibilities in the master's house, can look in vain for a line that says she even exists. Nobody means to slight her—heavens no! It isn't that she isn't "fit to print"; she just isn't important enough to be considered news.

This is bound to be a jolt for her, for formerly, where family life was everything, this now even-unmentioned woman was a good-sized frog in their private puddle. The little puddle might now have expanded into a large one, but her role in it had shrunk appreciably. It was Yale's puddle now, and part of a master's wife's job was to keep her family affairs under wraps as far as possible, and see to it that they did not intrude in any way on those of the college. The reason the family was there at all was to watch out for the concerns of the boys; the boys, not our family, were to be paramount. As a mother, my first duty had been to my children; but now, as a master's wife, my first duty was to the boys of his college, and our children would have to be shunted to second place. I should be successful here only if I remembered that constantly, and *liked it that way*. No kicking against the pricks!

The next major change for me was the uneasy knowledge that there was no *safety* here. Keys, keys, those blasted keys. Everything had to be kept locked. I went to my sewing machine and stitched up a stout little canvas pocket in which to keep this horrendous keyring, which I was cautioned never to be without. A narrow leather belt slipped into the hem at the top, and I buckled on this holster when I dressed in the morning. Having a "holster mother" delighted the children, who were just then Gene Autry fans, and they pretended that the bulky lump that filled it was not a keyring but a revolver. Those keys weighed heavily not only on my hip, but also on my mind, with the constant locking up necessary. Whenever I made a simple trip to the basement pantry to bring up a new supply of anything, it meant unlocking and relocking four doors. The laundry must always be kept locked, for fear the things spread on the drying racks would be made off with by someone who had managed to get through an outside gate and then through a basement door. In the country everything had swung free on the backyard clothesline, with no risk whatever of being taken. I could even go away from the house while airing expensive woolen blankets or winter clothes, with the certainty that they would still be there when I returned. Not in town.

The Branford garage opened on High Street sidewalk, but there was also an inside door into the basement stairs, and thus to the kitchen. In North Haven, we kept the car in the unlocked barn, and often I didn't even close the big doors when I came in. Here I had to leave the car half in the street, half across the sidewalk, while I got out and unlocked and pushed up the overhead door, then later pulled it down and locked it after me. On one of the few times that I didn't do this right away, I returned to find a grimy little man filling a gunnysack with Coca-Cola empties waiting to be picked up. The little man had beat them to it.

Not only was all this constant locking up a great nuisance, but living behind barricaded doors and in constant distrust of everyone was wearing. It was a comfort to know that the headquarters of the campus police was just across High Street, but a worry to know that their presence was necessary, which on this downtown street it certainly was. Both day and night, light-fingered passersby gently tried our door "just in case." Hoodlums in teenage gangs, or alone, and as young as ten years old, in broad daylight and while people were passing, constantly investigated the student bicycle racks along the sidewalk to see if one had been left unlocked. Sometimes they even removed an unchained front or back wheel and carried it off. The children didn't carry keys, of course, but they had to learn about the necessity of keeping night latches on.

I hated to have to be instilling into the children at such an early age a distrust of every stranger, but it had to be done. One day our middle little daughter was skating up and down on the sidewalk right in front of the house, and getting too warm, she pulled off her little corduroy jacket and dropped it on our front steps. She was never out of sight of it, but as she skated away, her back was turned. Someone walking by snatched it up and stuffed it inside his coat. When she got back from skating down to the corner, it was gone.

There were a number of High Street characters who were perfectly harmless, such as "Fi' Buck," a man who hung around Yale station, ready to buy any cast-off student clothes, and holding up five fingers as the price he was ready to pay. Another was the old Russian who sold shoelaces at the entrance to the Old Campus. He knew no English, but smiled and bobbed at passersby. Winter and summer, he wore an overcoat reaching to his heels and buttoned to his chin—perhaps nothing under it. One sweltering day I made the humanitarian mistake of taking a cold Coca-Cola over to him. In gratitude, he immediately crossed the street and took up his stand on our front steps, which became from that time onward his regular place of business. No one could go in or out of our door without having a tray of shoelaces thrust under his nose. As a result, I eventually accumulated a supply on hand to last the family a lifetime, of all colors and lengths.

But there were also people walking on High Street with more sinister motives. One day while I was in the court I was surprised to see through the kitchen windows two men moving around inside. The plumber had been going in and out the back door earlier to get tools from his truck, but I thought rightly that he had been gone several hours, the door locked behind him. Just then the window was opened, and Mr. Shea, one of the "campus cops" and our very good friend, called and asked me to come inside. Another man was standing in the kitchen with him.

"Do you know this man?" Mr. Shea asked me, indicating the second person.

"Should I?" I countered, thinking perhaps he was a returned alumnus, playing that stupid little game of I'll Bet You Don't Know Who I Am. "I don't believe I do. I can't recall ever having seen him before."

"He says he is your cousin, here on a visit to you. I saw him fiddling with your kitchen door lock, and followed him in. He was going up your back stairs."

My self-styled cousin, on being searched, was found to have half a dozen wristwatches in his pockets and a fat wallet of bills. Mr. Shea carried him away, and later telephoned to tell me that on the way to the police station he had been offered one of the watches and half the contents of the wallet (about $160) in exchange for freedom, whereupon this incorruptible Irishman promptly booked him on the additional charge of attempting to bribe an officer. When fingerprinted he was identified as a man wanted in three states. (Our back door *had* been locked, but he evidently needed no key. Clever kinfolks, mine!)

One of the differences about life in a city that smote me almost physically was NOISE. Several times each day nearby Park Street Firehouse Number 4 spewed forth a crimson monster to race shrieking down Elm Street. The citizens of New Haven *would* play with matches! A ladder stuck far out behind, with firemen clustered along it, struggling into heavy black slickers, clinging and bracing themselves as the truck with undiminished speed rounded the corners. Traffic scattered like autumn leaves before this clanging demon. Beside the helmeted driver crouched a magnificent dalmatian.

Less vociferous than the fire engines, but more numerous, were the trolley cars still running at that time at each end of our block. To get to and from classes, Yale boys jaywalked anywhere at all across Elm Street, apparently unconcerned about getting themselves killed, and the irate motorman often covered that block with his foot beating a steady tattoo on a resonant floor-gong. Elm and High were both two-way streets, and where they intersected there was no traffic light and a consequent medley of sound and confusion. Impatient automobile horns, the protesting screams of quickly braked tires when an accident was barely avoided, or the spine-chilling crash when it wasn't (there were two fatalities there our first year), exuberant and constant tootling from a procession of cars following a confetti-decked Italian wedding couple—about four a week of these—all seemed to be taking place practically in our front hall.

The children were ecstatic; for them it was pure heaven. They were delighted to hear it all; they wanted to go to the fire *and* the accident. What bliss if only two cars should crash at our front door! If only it could be our house that was on fire!

Even after vehicular traffic had quieted down for the night, there was no peace. Clump, clump, clump, went the big feet passing on the sidewalk. And no matter how late the hour, if a passing student happened on an empty beer can in the street he kicked it clanking all the way to the end of the block, where the next boy, coming the other way, would joyfully kick it back again. We got the full acoustical benefit of both trips.

I don't suppose I should class music as noise, but when it is not something you choose to sink into a chair and listen to, but instead something that, clashing and clanging, breaks willy-nilly into the peace of the day and assaults your ears whether you like it or not, I think it may be called noise. The heart of Yale is not a nest of singing birds, but it certainly is home to chiming bells and striking clocks.

While the great four-faced clock in the Harkness Tower directly over our heads did not strike, there were bells in the room at the tower's top to which an organist wound his way four times a day, then drew on thick gloves and manipulated the levers in the carillon's mechanism. At eight every morning his various selections probably called forth snarls from awakened student sleepers; at twelve noon he always played the same thing—the Largo from Dvorak's *New World Symphony*; at six, Wagner's bell motif from *Parsifal*; and at ten some Gregorian chant or a folk song to tell us all to sleep tight, and not let the mosquitoes bite. The poignant melody of Dvorak's "Going Home" played at noon every day probably touches a nostalgic note for many men hearing it in later years, far from Yale, remembering that rendering in their student days. I'll grant that the Harkness bells are music, not noise, but they do beat on the eardrums.

Across the street was Battell, the college chapel, with a large outside clock that did not play tunes but *struck*, forcefully and often, not only the hours but the quarters as well, with one boom for each of them, then the correct number of booms for the hour. When it was twelve, whether midday or midnight, it took the clock so long to finish telling the fact that the internal mechanism was already rattling around in its throat setting up the next quarter hour.

When you were wakened in the darkness of night to one solemn and very loud ear-splitting boom, figuring out what

41

time that was telling was enough to keep you awake until it struck again. Had it been coming in on the tail-end of the one-o'clock proclamation, or was it the single and honest quarter-after-something-or-other hour, and if so, which one?

In the middle of the City Green, just a block away (we were either one or two blocks away from everything) Trinity Episcopal church played a hymn at noon on their chimes every weekday. A bank fronting on the Green had an electrical contrivance announcing noon each weekday with a folksong or patriotic air. Added to the burst of chiming and ringing at noon was the fact that it was also the hour at which all Yale morning classes ended, sending a moving mass of noisy students directly under our windows. The middle of the day was *not* "quiet hour"; twelve o'clock could be a cacophony of "Rejoice, ye pure in heart," "Annie Laurie," and "Going Home," plus a thundering army of passing feet.

During our first weeks in Branford I thought that those striking clocks and ringing bells would drive me insane. They did take a bit of getting used to, but after a while I began to regard them as a charming adjunct to life, a mellow-voiced friend calling to tell me through the daylight hours how the time was wagging, and in the night assuring me that all was well. On occasions when we went out of town, I really missed hearing them.

Not only did I have to get used to noise, but to *people*. So many of them, and at close range. I probably held a conversation with twenty people every day. I was used to only three, and they half-pint-sized ones, and to long blissful days of country silence in which alone to do my work and thinking. It was not that I loved man the less, but nature more.

Now the Branford secretary and several college aides were in the office all day until five, just a door away, banging away on typewriters and talking to each other and to other students who constantly popped in and out. Our back windows overlooked the largest of the courts, crossed six times a day by all the students who lived in the college, coming and going to meals. The front windows gave directly on busy High Street. Everywhere I looked, there were *people*. I wasn't used to so many, and so near.

Privacy was a word of which we knew not the meaning. Goldfish globes were cloistered monasteries compared to a master's house. It was a good thing that we led exemplary lives, for there were witnesses to every breath that any one of us drew. Often in the living room in the evening we looked up to see a student in the doorway. He had come through the office, found nobody (naturally, since the secretary went home at five), knocked, called, and when no one answered, just kept coming until he found us.

Problems in students' lives do not confine themselves to office hours of nine to five, and we liked for them to feel free to come at any time that they needed to. And they certainly did. They ate a little earlier than we did in the evening, and often a boy coming to ask some question after his dinner found us still at ours. Pulling up a chair and having another plate and fork brought in at dessert time was a common occurrence.

The doorbell rang constantly; we hadn't even had one in North Haven. Milk and the newspaper had been simply "left," and unless the rural mail carrier had a package too large to go in our box by the roadside, Steve, returning from the college, was often the only person who came to the house all day. If anyone else did come, rapping knuckles, or a friendly "Anybody home?" sufficed.

Now I was amazed that so many people, instead of attending to their own business in their own homes or offices where they belonged, felt that they must tear around, to "post o'er land and ocean without rest," managing en route to come by our irresistible doorbell. This meant that for me there could be no more ranging comfortably around the house in the mornings in a rumpled smock; I must always be suitably dressed to answer these insistent peals, for it might be one of our old boys back—and they were always welcome, no matter at what hour.

Once one of them came about eleven-thirty, after we were in bed. Steve answered the door in a bathrobe, and I heard him greeting warmly one of our last year's graduates, now in the navy at a Florida base. "Had an unexpected two-day leave, sir, and just flew up."

They talked for at least an hour, and when the navy man was at the door leaving, Steve happened to say, "Where are you staying, George?"

There was an awkward pause, and then the two men came laughing up the stairs, George carrying his duffle bag. He stayed with us until his leave was up.

But a ring at the bell didn't always bring such a welcome visitor. It was much more apt to be an earnest soul who callously took up time, trying to get me to join some organization for the prevention, promotion, promulgation, or propagation of something or other. My simple statement, straight from the heart, that people who lived in this house didn't have time to join things, was not as convincing to solicitors as it was to me. Sometimes the bell-ringer had a child along. That usually meant Jehovah's Witnesses, and I delighted in seeing their amazement when I told them I read the entire Bible through when I was twelve years old. (It is the truth, too. It was for a Sunday school contest, and I won a prize for doing it.) My bell-ringers were quite often sales-people offering insurance, snow tires, hot panholders; a delivery man at the wrong address; service bureau men to fix something out of kilter; a member of the faculty making a shortcut through the house to Steve's office.

But welcome or far from it, it was all very time-consuming, and when it turned out to be an idle person with time to kill (something I never was), simply looking for someone to talk to and who found me easily get-at-able, it was a blasted nuisance. One day a childless faculty wife, living at the Lawn Club without a care in the world, prefaced her hour-long call on a lovely fall afternoon with this tactless statement: "The weather was so beautiful that I simply had to take a short walk. 'Now, who do I know,' I asked myself, 'who lives nearby?' I racked my brain, and finally I thought of you."

At one period, when the deluge of bell-ringers had been especially heavy, I had the brilliant idea of making a mask, perhaps of putty, or paper mâché, and coloring it a hideous blue. If I wore this, people checking the ward for Demo-cratic voters or asking what radio program I was listening to when the bell rang might be gone more promptly.

Eventually, I came up with the perfect solution, and it was much less trouble than making a mask. It was to keep a hat on the hall sofa, and before answering the door, put it on. I could then say breathlessly, "Oh, I'm so sorry; I'm just going out—late to an appointment." Or if it were a welcome visitor, I would whip the hat off and say, "I'm just coming in; so glad you caught me!"

The children adored answering the bell. From their contact with the world the shy little country mice became overnight not always, I regret to say, the charming and helpful children I had envisaged, but sometimes uppity little overconfident juveniles who instead of delivering messages took it upon their utterly incompetent shoulders to deal with whatever situation had come up. Here are a couple of examples.

The scholarly, severe-looking former secretary of the university—whose very appearance I should have thought would have inspired awe in any bosom, it certainly did in mine—rang the bell one Saturday afternoon during an exciting moment in a Yale-Cornell football game being played in Ithaca. The door burst open in his face, he was seized by a firm, eight-year-old grip and dragged into the living room, then pushed into a chair beside the radio.

"Don't say a word," a stern young Yale fan admonished him. "It's 13–13, Yale's ball, and two minutes to play in the last quarter."

Mr. Stokes sat obediently speechless until the final whistle, and not before then was he allowed to state that his business was with Steve. He was told that the Master of Branford had gone to Ithaca with the team.

On another Saturday afternoon a tired father warned three noisy children to keep quiet, saying that he intended to have the peace of a nap interrupted by *no one*, "unless," he added, "the king of England calls."

In the course of the next half-hour Senator Robert Taft,

then candidate for the presidential nomination and in town for a meeting of the Yale corporation, came by to see my husband about something. A small girl answered his ring, opened the door a slim crack, and applied a cold eye to it.

"Is your father in?"

"Who are you? Are you the king of England?"

"Thank heaven, no."

"Then you can't see him. He is taking a nap, and he told us not to wake him for anybody but the king of England." And the door was firmly closed in the face of a man whose father had been president of the United States and who had himself at that time a very good chance of becoming the next one.

6

*C*ertainly one of the greatest joys of my new manner of living was being under the wing of the university service bureau, a corps of carpenters, painters, masons, plumbers, electricians, groundsmen, workmen of all sorts, experts in every facet of building management, skilled and friendly *and free*, who took care of all of us living at the university. If anything broke, or didn't seem to be working quite as it should, or began to wobble or smoke or drip, just a telephone call and presto! one of these men was right there. They showed up sometimes when we hadn't even given them a call, just to check on how something was working. Being themselves the ones who installed the thing in the first place, they knew all about whatever it was, and so brought along with them a tool kit in which was everything they might need, never having to resort to the usual practice of all paid-by-the-job workmen of leaving everything torn up in non-working confusion while they go back for a part, or write to the place in Wisconsin where it is manufactured. They were another inroad upon our privacy, of course, for they came in anywhere at any time, but they were one intrusion that we gladly accepted. Would anyone resent a plumber's entrance when the basement was two feet under water? People in private homes could stand at the top of their cellar stairs and watch the waters rising below because the plumber they called "put them on his list, but couldn't promise any definite date"; we had only to keep a finger in the dyke for the time it took a man to come from Ashmun Street on the double. Workmen were constantly buzzing around fixing things we didn't know were even there, much less needed repairing. They were as much at home as we were, more so really, for they took care of this place before we came, and would continue to do it after we left.

They walked calmly and imperturbably around, doing what had to be done, paying no attention whatever to us, and I soon learned to treat them in the same way, but it took a little getting used to, for an unexpected encounter with one could be rather a shock.

Soon after we moved in, I was splashing away one day in our second floor bathroom, behind the drawn shower curtain, when I thought I heard someone in the room. I parted the curtains, and presented an inquiring face to the upper half of a man framed in the open window.

"Don't let me startle you," he caroled cheerily, "I'll be through here in a minute."

It was one of the groundsmen, who, strolling through the court, had noticed a wisteria vine that had pulled loose from the wall, so he had brought a ladder and was fastening it back. It just happened to be outside my bathroom, and I just happened to be taking a shower.

They were superb workmen in everything, and had all the best equipment. Floors they waxed gleamed like the Hall of Mirrors, and one's life and limbs weren't worth a dime on them. An elderly friend, calling soon after one of their floor-waxing visits, made the remark, "Anyone with floors as slippery as these should provide a house surgeon."

While we were off on a summer holiday, they came over and washed all our woodwork, leaving it gleamingly clean, and the children's heights and weights that I had marked on the inside of a closet door and guarded for years were gone forever.

When the masons were knocking into the stone work to repair a chipped place, or mending the copper gutters, or the pipes, a wham-banging went on that carried not only into every part of the building but right straight into your eye-teeth. The summer that I had a major operation, and we didn't get away to our country home until August, they repointed the whole quadrangle—six floors, tower and all—and the steady African drumbeat of the masons' hammers kept up all day long for over a month. We got to where we talked, ate, walked, thought to the rhythm.

My first introduction to the men of the service bureau came only a few days after we had moved in, when I had driven out on an errand and, coming back, attempted to fit the station wagon into its new home.

The Branford garage was tucked into the building just beyond the kitchen, with its door on High Street. I had formerly been used to driving with careless grace and one finger through big barn double doors built to accommodate a loaded hay wagon. Now I had to slide tidily into a city garage space that fitted like a glove.

The entrance looked very, very narrow to me, but this was the house garage, and I was in the car that was hence-forth to live in that little cupboard, so I gritted my teeth and pointed the nose of the car at it. With city traffic honking

impatiently behind me to hurry, hurry, and taxis darting out
of line to pass me (even after I had signaled a left turn, both
with the turning light and by pointing my arm out of the
window, wagging it and almost getting it taken off), I had to
make a perfect swing from the street directly into this rabbit-
hole. The results were shattering, literally; there was the
most horrendous crash. I expected the whole building to
totter.

If the cartoons over which people roar with laughter are
to be believed, plenty of women drivers do this all the time.
But in the quiet and seclusion of one's own backyard, what
does it matter if by a little easily understandable miscalcula-
tion you take off the door, or go out through the back of the
building? Whanging to pieces part of a massive stone building on a busy street is another thing, not to speak of the
ghastly publicity of it all, for at least a hundred students in
the dormitory across the street rushed to their windows and
cheered. The fortresslike building didn't collapse, of course,
for all I had done was rip off a door facing, but I had to call
the service bureau to confess and to ask for someone to repair
it.

Two days later, I did it again—to the facing on the other
side of the door this time, for I was shying away from my
former crash. Again my service bureau friend replaced it.

A week later, when it happened for the third time, I
stood by in humiliation while he took out his tape and
measured the width, first of the car, and then of the door
opening.

"Now don't you worry over this," he said comfortingly,
"You're not such a bad driver. You've only got four inches on
each side to make it. The ordinary clearance in a garage is

twelve." What a whale of a lot of difference those missing inches made to a driver used to a barn door.

The overhead garage door, in keeping with the architecture of the rest of the building, was medieval, made of "heart of oak," resembling a portcullis, and heavy enough to resist any enemy's battering ram. It weighed about a ton, and really should have been raised and lowered by a couple of stout yeomen turning a windlass, rather than by the frail arm of one woman, but the crash of my entrance, while embarrassing, at least used to bring to the scene enough students to help me get the heavy door down. When I became so accustomed to the tight turn-in that I could maneuver it without any attendant crash, my audience fell away, and unable to pull the door down alone, I had to have a motor installed to do it.

A VISIT from the service bureau usually started with a ring at the back door. There stood a man with a yellow work slip in his hand.

"I've come to repair the So-and-So," he said.

It may have been news to me that the So-and-So wasn't functioning properly, but perhaps the office secretary or my husband had discovered and reported it, so I invited him in. He could come in anyway, via the office or basement, and was ringing out of pure politeness.

My best service bureau story started out like this. A friend had come up from Georgia on a visit, and when she arrived was quite exhausted from the long trip. After the first greetings, we decided that a short nap before lunch would be the best thing for her. There was just time. "Only a short lie-down with my eyes closed," she said, "and I'll be fine."

I took her up to the southwest guest-room, the end room in the house, and the farthest away from all household noises. She hadn't been there ten minutes when the doorbell rang.

It was a workman from the service bureau with a helper, both with heavy tool kits over their shoulders.

"We've come about that door."

I had no idea anything was wrong with any of our doors, but when a workman stands on the doormat, and says he is here to fix something, no one in her senses would send him away.

"Any particular door?"

He consulted his yellow work slip. "In the southwest bedroom."

That was the room in which Gertrude was having her lie-down with her eyes closed. It was too bad, but I hope I know better than to tell a willing and ready workman to come back another time because someone is taking a nap, so I ushered them both upstairs.

As we entered the room, I explained in a quiet, offhand manner to my startled friend, upended on her elbow at our entrance, that these men were only going to do a little hammering and sawing, and for her to pay no attention to them and go on with her nap. She did not seem to be completely convinced, but at least lay back down. By that time I had lived here long enough so that having two brawny workmen in the room with destructive tools they planned to use wouldn't have interrupted a particle of any rest I might be taking with my eyes closed, but Gertrude, unused to life in a master's house, seemed a little bothered. I think she kept her eyes open so that she could leap to avoid a blow if she saw it coming, so I stayed around to reassure her that everything was perfectly all right. The way I figured it was that they were here, and were going, willy-nilly, to get to work on what they came for, so there was no reason to be upset.

They unslung their tool kits and began selecting mallets and hammers; then they pushed some furniture around. The main man stood back and looked at the south wall, and then looked at a blueprint he had along, and said, "About here," and took a pencil and made a mark.

To let them know how delighted I was to have them taking care of the whole thing, whatever it was, I said in a chatty, conversational tone, but not loud enough to bother Gertrude in case she had dozed off, "I'm afraid I didn't know anything about any door. Do you mind telling me who sent in the order?"

He consulted his yellow slip again. "The master."

So! Well, wait until I got my hands on him! Of course, by this time I should have been accustomed to having things like this happen. He had accepted the master's appointment before he had even let me know that it had been offered, and had the foundation of a new garage laid before it occurred to him to tell me that the project at our summer home that year was not to be the often-talked-of tennis court. I had to keep reminding myself that he had been a bachelor, deciding things himself alone, for a long time before he was a family man, so he kept on forgetting about me, and that I might like to be in on weighty decisions. He had bought the house in

North Haven that was supposed to be our home for the rest of our lives before I had even seen the inside. The owners were never at home when I came on an inspection trip with him, so he just went ahead and bought it anyway, calmly telling me that he knew I would like it as much as he did. (And he was right; I did, perhaps even more so.) But to send men to knock a great hole in a wall in the house we were living in, without even saying "boo" to me about it, was really the limit.

The workman tested the heft of a mallet and decided against it; he picked out a heavier one.

"You are very lucky," he went on. "We are going to cut a door through this wall, and take in the room on the other side for your new baby." He raised his mallet for a mighty blow.

Now, my lord and master might do things like buy a home, build a garage, and take on a new job without consulting me, but at least I had been in on all the new babies in the family. I stopped the workman just before his mallet crashed into the wall.

"Hold on! Before you go irreparably any further, there are two things you ought to know. One is that I haven't had a new baby for five years, and the other is that there isn't any room beyond that wall. It is an *outside* wall."

He looked at me in absolute horror.

"Would that little work slip of yours for the new door be, by any chance, for number 90 High Street, instead of 80?"

He consulted it.

"Why, yes, it is. Isn't this the Saybrook master's house?" he asked in surprise.

I gave him the response we used to make when as children we played Pussy-wants-a-corner: "Next door neighbor."

Quite embarrassed, they gathered up their tools and departed to wreak their destruction and improvement at number 90, next door, for the benefit of the Saybrook master's new baby. And my friend had a story to take back to Georgia about the unbelievable things that went on in Yankee houses.

7

Our dog and cat found no silver lining in their town life. Everything was a bit more awkward for them than in their former existence—or at least, I found their living here that. Many of the plans for them that we and Yale had concocted together did not work out quite as ideally as we had expected and hoped they would.

Every fair day that was not too cold I carried the cat, poor helpless creature, into the large wire cage that I had had made for him in the moat, where anyone walking down High Street sidewalk might look over the wall with a pitying eye at this proud-spirited soul, ignominiously caged. He always crouched down immediately in the ivy with his back towards me, probably cursing me roundly in cat language. Apparently he took no advantage of the fresh air to do any calisthenics, for he was always in exactly the same spot and position when I went to bring him in at dusk.

This cat trip called for the use of several keys on my ring; it meant unlocking the kitchen to back stairs door, going down the nineteen steps to the basement, then a 171-foot trek along basement halls, unlocking doors as I went, the last one being the outside door into the moat. Then I went through it all in reverse back into the house, with the whole procedure to do again when it was time to bring him in. Unlike the children, who adored the scary basement rooms reminiscent of fairy tale castle dungeons, I did not rejoice in traversing them twice daily. And I always had to keep poor Percy on my mind, for the whole time he was outside, too, for there was no shelter in case it rained.

During the years that we were there I added up all the figures involved and it came out that I made this trip 14,440 times, which amounted to traveling 3,062,400 feet on the level (which is 580 miles), and 27,300 stair steps, the equivalent of climbing to the top of the Washington Monument and back down 149 times. All to fill that cat's lungs with the fresh air he neither needed nor wanted.

Nancy's daily care was different, but even more of a problem, for dogs do need to be exercised, and have to have more than a litter box for a bathroom. When she indicated that she felt she was on the wrong side of an outside door, it was necessary, without too much delay, for someone to get her to the right side. In the court, under the kitchen windows, was the tiny walled-in corner, termed "Nancy's yard," for necessary trips outside, but getting there took too much time—going the length of the Pullman-strung-out house inside, through the office, through the outside entry hall door, back down the court to walk the length of the house again, and then unbolting the little wall door to her yard. No dog in Christendom could be expected to wait so long! Also, the length of the court that we would have had to traverse was overlooked by about a hundred boys' rooms, and sometimes Nancy chose to go out when we were not dressed, or in the middle of the night, or when it was pouring rain. For a while we were in such despair over this situation that we thought we might have to give her up, which none of us could bear the thought of.

Then, in desperation, we hit on an arrangement that we admitted was ridiculous, but it worked. We got the same amenable carpenter who had constructed Percy's cage—by now amazed and bewildered at the preposterous things we were asking him to rig up for our pets—to make Nancy a lightweight ramp, with cleats so her claws wouldn't slip, which when not in use would stand up against the kitchen wall out of the way, and which, whenever Nancy indicated that she needed to go, could quickly be hooked over the rim of the sink counter. The window was then opened, and the little dog walked up the ramp and out of the window. Outside there was a small platform from which another ramp led to the ground. This was stained an inconspicuous brown so that it blended with the stone building and was not too noticeable. When she was ready to come in again, she came up the outside ramp, seated herself on the platform, and presented a piteous face, even occasionally letting out an impatient yip to be let back in. Whenever it snowed, one of us would go out and shovel this ramp and platform off with the pancake turner. Every day, with a scooper, I cleaned up the space outside.

When shown this arrangement guests went into whoops of laughter, but as I said, it worked. It took a little while, and a great deal of patience, pushing and prodding, to get Nancy to understand her part in all this and what the ramps were for. Then there was explaining to each new cook I had during the next ten years about her part in the performance.

But Nancy was a winsome bitch, and won over most cooks very soon. Moving the lightweight ramp into place and removing it later wasn't really too much trouble.

Some member of the family, or a student, usually managed to take Nancy for a walk around the block every day for exercise. Boys usually like dogs, and since students were not allowed to keep any of their own in their rooms, they eagerly adopted ours. But there was no more running free for her. She had never seen a leash before, but now we bought her one, and she never went out again, except to her little yard under the kitchen windows, without it.

There was one time when wanderlust proved too much for her, and she edged unnoticed between the butter-and-egg man's legs at the back door when he was making a delivery, and for six days she explored New Haven on her own. All of the family, campus cops, and helpful students combed the district for her in vain—a little black cocker shadow had disappeared. Buckets of tears flowed at our house. At the end of a heartbroken week, in answer to an ad that we had been running in the newspaper "lost" column, two little boys appeared at the front door with the forlorn culprit. They had picked her up, wandering around Wooster Square, half a mile across town, ravenous and thirsty, dirty and smelly beyond words, her lovely black curls matted with chewing gum. In her joy of being home, she almost ate us up and, a thorough penitent, she never ran away again.

So much for the dog and cat. The children were another matter.

8

*H*ow fared our children in this new setup? A good question, to which there was not always a good answer.

Those masters' houses which had been planned as such on an architect's drawing board had been given private gardens. (The one at Berkeley was walled, not overlooked, and with a charming little summerhouse.) But Branford and Saybrook, contrived out of an already existing building, had none. Of all the colleges, their courts are the most beautiful, but their masters' houses paid a price for this. The courts were laid out for formal display, and are far from being a cosy family retreat to privacy. The master and his entourage, which certainly included any children he might happen to have, were placed there to provide a little touch of family life to this otherwise ideal monastic existence, but that life had to go on indoors.

The administration knew when we came in that we had children, and made no objection as long as they were not too obstreperous—in other words, were neither seen nor heard. No tearing around and shouting; it would disturb boys trying to study behind the many windows that overlooked the courts. No shrieks of "You're it!" and "You can't catch me!" and such. And above all, whatever they did they must adhere to the rule already laid down, not just for them, but for the students as well, to *Keep Off the Grass!* No foot, large or small, masculine or feminine, was to profane that sacred turf!

To the romantic poets, a blade, stepped upon, would spring back from the pressure of a feminine footfall, but in real life, this just wasn't so. Instead, the flattened blade simply gave up the ghost, turned brown and died—and that must never happen to a single blade in the Branford court-yard. Those grassy squares were the pride of Yale, to which visitors were always brought, and in order to keep them in their perfect condition, solicitous groundsmen hovered over them, tweaking out any incipient dandelion plant while it was still floating in the air as a seed parachute, keeping grass blades mowed to just the right uniform height. Oxford and Cambridge groundsmen are said to tell visitors that the simple way they produce their velvety quads is merely to roll them and mow them for several hundred years. We didn't have those centuries behind us, so we had to make up for them by constant and meticulous supervision.

The little girls were allowed to use one tiny secluded cobblestone corner of a court, but only if they played there quietly with their dolls and were sure to bring back into the house everything they took out. When the daily tour of the university came through, the courtyard must not look like the vinegar works.

The children experimented with a few other things besides dolls, such as rolling hoops, but found it was impossible not to succumb to the excitement of racing each other, with consequent squeals. A runaway hoop could easily wobble off the walk and crash into a flower-bed.

Occasionally they turned a jump rope on the flagstone walk, and invited boys on the way to the dining hall to jump through. Most of them nimbly complied; only a few walked around with a scowl and muttered something about "brats." Many boys had small sisters of their own, and they enjoyed seeing the children around. These boys would give the girls chewing gum or slow up for a few minutes' chat when they encountered them walking the dog or skating.

The children had learned to rollerskate in the cement-floored basement rooms. The walks in the court were flagstones, impossible for skating, and besides, skates would make too much clackety racket there. But we were surrounded by city sidewalks, and if they never crossed a street and turned right at every corner, they had a whole square block on which to skate around in safety, although, I suspect, to the annoyance of pedestrians. But they had to play somewhere.

They were surrounded with more thou-shalt-nots than the ancient Hebrews. They were never, of course, to go into a student entry, nor into the Common Room. I tried to get all the prohibitions firmly in their minds before they could break them, for they never disobeyed if something had been forbidden, but I couldn't always think of things before they did. It never occurred to me, for instance, to say they were not to go up on the roof, any more than to tell them the good old literary New England standby of not to put beans up their noses.

One afternoon while they were playing dolls in their corner of the court, one of them wondered aloud what the world looked like from the top of the towers. A grand idea, and one that had not been forbidden. No sooner thought of than attempted. Dolls tucked under arms, obeying the commandment about never leaving anything in the court, they climbed an open fire escape to what is called the Jewel Tower, which was six stories above the street. At its top there was an open platform, protected only by two iron rails, with no banisters. Here they found a deck chair that some sunbathing student had left. Each little girl wanted to climb into it, and in the ensuing scuffle the chair crashed over the edge to the sidewalk below, barely missing a pedestrian.

A campus policeman happened to be passing at the time, and appeared in Steve's office with the shattered chair and an account of what had happened. A badly frightened father went out in the court in time to meet three even more badly frightened children who were clambering, white-faced, down the fire escape—and who never set foot on a fire escape again.

Carefree, unsupervised play days—the best kind—were over. Wherever they were now, some grown person's eye, often mine, had to be on them every minute.

The playground that the university had pulled out of a hat, and that we had thought would solve all our problems, proved to be only another problem. To begin with, it was three busy street crossings away, so the girls could only go there when someone was free to take them there and stay with them. It is not good for healthy, intelligent children never to be able to go anywhere on their own, but always to have to be taken. However, for this purpose, the high school would often send me a girl to go with them for the afternoons. This helper did indeed, like the gazelle in the song, "glad me with her soft brown eye," but also like the gazelle, "when I came to know her well, and love her, she was sure to"—not die certainly, but expire for me. For she would get a job in a store, or at the library, or become a candystriper at the hospital, and the children would be left house-bound again.

There was also no safe, enclosing fence at the playground, and my children frequently found older boys in possession of it—often pugnacious street arabs who soared high in their swings with no intention of ever getting out— and my little girls would have to retreat and leave the interlopers pumping away. City cats gloried in the sandbox, so that was useless to us; someone had always tilted the cover off between our visits there.

There were no homes anywhere near us but the masters' houses, and most of them had no children at all, or as Tercia had written of the Smith children next door, they were "groan," and useless as playmates for ours. What would we have done without the college guards at the gateways, and the campus cops? The business of a guard was just to sit there, with nothing to do but be bored to death, and he would often be good-natured enough to welcome having a little girl or two perched on his desk chattering to him. The children also idolized the campus police and paid many a call at their headquarters on the Old Campus. At Halloween the girls reduced those staunch gentlemen to a very satisfactory condition of terror by calling on them as little ghosts and red devils. The campus cop would be one of their happiest memories of growing up in that childless neighborhood.

This dearth of nearby children was hard on us all. I was not a flinty-hearted mother, willing to see my bairns confined in solitary grandeur within these palace walls. As they grew older I constantly drove hither and yon, taking them to play with school friends living in other parts of town, or bringing those children to 80 High Street, and arranging things they could do indoors. April, the month in which they were all three born, was top-heavy with birthday celebrations. We had spiderweb parties for which I crawled around for hours beforehand tangling up the entire house in balls of colored twine, weaving it in and out of chair legs and banisters, looping it around door knobs—a fire would have had us all toasted to a crisp before we could ever have gotten out. Remembering the candy-pulls we had in my own youth, I gave one once for the entire third grade in the cement-floored laundry, where dropped dollops would not be as catastrophic as they might be upstairs. While the taffy was boiling, the little boys became so fascinated by the automatic clothes washer and the dumbwaiter, and investigated their workings so thoroughly, that it took a couple of men from the service bureau half a day to get them operating smoothly again.

For much of the time, of course, our girls were dependent only on themselves for entertainment. An only child would have had a sad life at Branford, but three siblings together can usually manage to have a wonderful time, and ours assuredly did.

There was at first, indoors, the excitement and intoxication of exploring a new home, and a castle at that. The huge bare basement rooms divided by heavy fire doors which took their combined strength to push aside were deliciously frightening, quite as satisfactory as any medieval dungeon. They were never supposed to go in these basement rooms without an adult along, but this was one place where my usually obedient little angels often circumvented me. Their most delightful indoor adventure was to slip down the kitchen stairs to the basement, making a first stop at the college janitor's cleaning closet, where each armed herself with a mop or broomstick, "just in case they met anything," and then wend a circuitous way to the room where the contents of the students' wastebaskets was compacted. If they could get there when there was a good-sized accumulation, they would sort through it all as avidly as any old street bag lady, and come back with all sorts of junk, discarded by the students but treasures to them, which then had to be kept hidden in the playroom cupboards since its source could not be admitted. After they reached school age these surreptitious treasure hunts were one of the delights which their schoolmates joyously shared with them when they came to play for an afternoon.

Another was demonstrating the electric dumbwaiter by sending dolls up and down. Two sides of the waiter were safely closed, but the other two were simply cavernous open spaces, which meant that everything must be carefully kept away from the edges, for when the button was pressed and the conveyance started its trip, anything that touched the edge would be scraped off by the wall and torn into shreds or smithereens before it reached its destination. I was terrified that in spite of reiterated stern warnings some daring child would double up inside for a ride, and get a leg or an arm removed. Waiting for the safe arrival of dolls was not half as thrilling as the passage of a live passenger would have been. As far as I know, though, they never did try it.

The lack of neighborhood children was a real sorrow, for three was not enough to constitute a real gang, but the girls managed pretty well. Prima organized and directed plays and tableaux innumerable for every season, with their father, the maid, Nancy, Percy, and I as audience. Since there were only three members of her cast, when there had to be more characters she would requisition chairs for nonspeaking parts. Father Joseph in the Nativity scene each year was always a chair wearing Steve's striped bathrobe as an authentic Eastern costume, and angels were a bevy of chairs draped in sheets.

After they started school the girls were entranced with the idea of classroom discipline, and often carried on an afternoon session in the playroom, with the oldest girl a delightfully horrid teacher, dealing out both assignments and punishments to her two pupils with a heavy hand. After a siege of chicken pox they used the dolls for patients, and turned the playroom into a hospital ward, and themselves into nurses. Rigged out in short ruffled stand-out skirts that I made out of white mosquito netting, they were ballet dancers, using the upstairs stair rail as the bar. The office secretary brought them a discarded sample book of ladies' stationary that she got hold of somewhere, and they ripped out the samples and wrote letters to all of the family on notepaper headed Mrs. Donald G. Montgomery, 182 Jacinta Avenue, Pasadena, California; Mrs. Angela K. Cox, 196 Astor Place, Philadelphia; and many others, and dropped them through the mail slot in the front door.

The oldest girl, Prima, had her own library card, and could amuse herself for hours by reading. The middle daughter, Secunda, from the time she could hold a crayon, had always been perfectly contented if she had a piece of paper to draw on. But the youngest child, Tercia, could do neither of these two things, and while the other two were happily engaged in reading and drawing, she was often miserably lonely. When the time came that both the older girls were in school, and Tercia was left alone at home, her playmateless mornings became really desolate. She was devoted to our dog and cat, willingly brushing and combing them, and proud when I let her put the leash on Nancy and walk her up and down the block. But two animals were not enough. She loved every living creature she met up with anywhere. One day I found her happily chattering to and affectionately petting the milkman's horse, a dreadful wall-eyed creature that was wrinkling up his lips and showing huge yellow teeth that looked quite capable of crushing a caressing hand. Horrified, I snatched my child to safety, in spite of her protest: "But, Mother, he wouldn't bite *me!*"

Every night at the end of her prayers, when she had finished calling down blessings on the prescribed family members, "all God's children everywhere," and a list of her own favorites among the students and campus cops, for years she would add earnestly, "And please, dear God, don't forget to send a pony to 80 High Street." A few doors up the hall I was just as earnestly countermanding the order: "God, don't you dare do any such thing!"

Fortunately my prayers, not hers, were answered, but a child who loved animals so passionately really had to be allowed to own a few. For two years we had a bright-eyed little hamster who used to get out of his cage and hide in impossible places all over the house. Goldfish have swum in and out of our lives, but they were unsatisfactory—you can't pet a goldfish—and for a short while there was a canary. I could not bear the idea of a caged bird ("A robin redbreast in a cage puts all Heaven in a rage") and would not have one in the house, but a Branford Fellow brought Tercia a pretty little canary, and she was so overjoyed that I weakly let her keep it. She didn't like the idea of its being caged, either, and was constantly letting it out to fly around her room. One day a window was open a slit, and the little blob of yellow sensed the fresh air, and flew through to freedom. The bird and I rejoiced, but the little girl wept.

Once a company advertising something or other sent baby turtles through the mail to Yale students. Most of them were immediately dumped in the Yale station wastebaskets, but about twenty boys brought theirs to Tercia, and for a few days our house crawled with the miniscule creatures. The time the poor little things had spent in transit sealed up in an envelope had fortunately shortened their lives, so that instead of having them grow to maturity and take over the whole house, we had the horror of watching them die, be enshrouded in newspaper, and be cremated in the basement incinerator.

Tercia wanted to bring home every stray dog and cat she met up with on city streets, to be fed and housed under our roof. In spite of her pleas I was adamant, for we simply could not start in again with a puppy or a kitten—not with Yale rugs on the floors, no yard, and city traffic rushing past our doors. Sometimes she succeeded in enticing a stray dog all the way to our door, and brought him in with a radiant introduction, "Look, Mother! He followed me home!" My heartless command that she take him right straight back and leave him exactly where she had met him always brought floods of tears.

The two older children were soon at the stage where other little girls of their own age were the only ones with whom they wanted to play, but Tercia wanted any companion at all, just so it breathed and preferably could talk, too—man, woman, or child; boys of any age, even rough, tough, and dirty ones, looked fine to her.

And she found companions. She stood in the open dining room windows and called to people going along the street, she scraped acquaintance with passersby when she went out to walk the dog around the block, even with the chronic bench-sitters on the Green with empty whiskey bottles lying on the grass beside them. All God's chillen were her friends, and the more she could enter into conversation with, the better. Dirt, germs, smells—her heart was big enough for them all. Mine wasn't.

One evening after dark a perfectly filthy little girl, about twelve, rang the bell. Her bitten fingernails were a combination of black dirt and peeling red nail polish. Her jaws were doing amazing things with a peculiarly sickening shade of pink bubblegum, her hair was stiff with dirt, and to my horrified eyes seemed to move with inhabitants as I gazed. She had come, she said, by invitation, to play with the little girl who lived here. I told her that seven o'clock was too late for my five-year-old to have company, and besides, she had already gone to bed.

"Is she just *five?*" the visitor demanded incredulously, bubblegum suspended between upper and nether millstones. "Well, I sure didn't know she wasn't no older than *that!*" She turned and departed in deep disgust.

One morning when I was putting the moated cat out I heard voices above me on the High Street sidewalk. They came from a group of tough little street boys, about ten or eleven years old. Our youngest daughter was right there in the midst of them, looking around with a beaming face. She had evidently been trying to ingratiate herself with them, but they were not sure they wanted her tagging along.

"Why, I bet you don't even know what ---- means," one of them had just said, using an indecent word found on boxcars and board fences sometimes. My child confessed with shame that she didn't.

"It's easy to see you ain't never went around with no gang of boys before," he said scornfully.

"No, but I'd *love* to!" breathed the master's little daughter.

Clean and sweet, lonely and utterly miserable, Tercia was bouncing a ball inside the big gate one day when another wandering boy passed on High Street and spied her. They got to talking through the gate, and finally he volunteered, "Say, I'll come in there and play with you. How do you get in?"

"You can't come in," she told him with sad finality. "They don't allow children to play in here."

"Well, you're there, ain't you? What are you doing in there for, then? How did you get in?"

"I live here, and I haven't anywhere else to go!" she cried, bursting into tears.

Looking out of the window one day I saw her in the court, deep in conversation with a gentleman in clerical collar and Church of England gaiters. Surely that is safe, I thought. A little later when I looked again they were still there, and Tercia was still yakking away for dear life, the gentleman apparently completely absorbed in what she was telling him.

"Heaven only knows what she was saying," I thought,

remembering some of her past disclosures, indiscreet to say the least, to perfect strangers that she sat beside on the bus on occasions when we could not get a seat together. "But he is a man of God, so I suppose it is all right. And he has legs; if he wants to escape, he can."

From time to time I looked out at them. She was still chattering steadily to an apparently rapt listener. They changed their positions occasionally, and the parson rested first one foot and then the other. Finally both must have given out, for he was propped against a tree, and she was sitting crosslegged on the ground at his feet, the ancient mariner still holding the wedding guest locked in conversation.

Finally I decided that I must rescue him. I gave a little ting to the bell that I used to call the children when I wanted them inside. Tercia waved to me, and after an earnest farewell to the priest, who staggered off, she scrambled to her feet and came trotting inside, beaming.

"What in the world did you find to talk to that man about for so long? Who was he, anyway?" I asked.

"Oh, a preacher from England," she answered airily. "He said 'hello' to me first, so of course I had to say 'hello' back. Then he started to tell me about English children where he lived, but I told him I knew all about them, because we had Mary Poppins, and Christopher Robin and Peter Pan and the Bastables and a lot more. But he didn't know anything at all about American children, so I was just telling him about them. I told him about Prima and Secunda, and everybody at Foote School and the teachers and Mrs. Sturley's jalopy that we went to the museum in, and Yale and you and father and everybody I could think of. He didn't know a thing before, but *now* he does," she finished complacently.

I am sure he did. I hoped that that voyageur talked to some other people on his visit to the United States, and did not form his entire conception of what Americans are like from my young daughter's glib tongue.

All in all, I suppose these children found life in the center of a city more exciting than the North Haven yard had been, but keeping a step ahead of them in town was certainly more exhausting for me.

9

$\mathcal{M}$y relatives were quite as curious as anybody else as to what went on behind the walls of this great stone castle, and what part I played, and they often asked me in their letters to tell them "in plain black and white," what do *you* do there? What are a master's wife's duties? Do you plan the college meals? Schedule their entertainments and social life? Are you a sort of Advice to the Lovelorn columnist, counseling students on their personal problems?

The answer to all of these is absolutely not. Not only was I not asked to do any of these things, but I was specifically told *not to*, and to keep hands off. The master's wife mustn't be a Meddlesome Matty. It might seem superfluous to have her around at all, but there was an unwritten rule that Yale masterships be given to married men; a wife was an unimportant piece of baggage that the important master was permitted to bring along. She lived in the house, but she had no duties to perform besides being housewife and hostess there, as she would in her own home. She wasn't a desk clerk, nor a consultant, nor any kind of organizer or supervisor. She had no set duties, no office hours—in fact, no office.

The college ran smoothly along with, at its heart, the master, his secretary, and several student aides. The dining hall was managed by a university-appointed dietitian and her staff. The other activities of the college, such as occasional plays, concerts, dances, a bulletin printed on a little press in the basement, and so on, were run by combined committees of students and faculty Fellows, under the master's guiding hand.

Athletics played a large part in every student's program; most of the boys were involved in some sport or other. There were so many things going on all the time in the various sports that few students were free to come out to these intramural games just as spectators, and there was where I could play a part. I went out to watch as many as I could sandwich in, cheering for "my team," running up and down the field following the play (a players' bench or two was usually the only grandstand for these games) and letting the boys see that the master's house was interested in what they do. If any player got hurt, I drove him over to the Field House and doctor, and when the game was over, I always had a carful of sweaty athletes and their equipment to bring back to the college. Some of them had cars, but not enough, and there were always grateful ride-thumbers.

So while theoretically I might sit on a cushion and stitch away at fine seams, a few things did turn up as the days passed that it was just as well I was around to take care of. Actually I did very little cushion-sitting. Here is a list of activities that one typical week brought:

The mother of a son in the infirmary with mononucleosis came to town to check on her son's illness. She had never known anyone who had that disease before, and was extremely upset. I calmed her down and persuaded her to stay a few days in our guest room, from which I could drive her up to see him every day during visiting hours, and around New Haven to see the sights at other times. (Although the New Haven tourist bureau never heard of me, I did a great deal of piloting people around their city.)

A West Coast alumnus on a business trip East brought his wife along to see his old stamping ground. They were both eager to see all the new things since he was a student here, so I took them on both a walking and driving tour of the whole university. While he was in his business sessions, she was at loose ends—in other words, she was all mine!

There was to be a wedding in the little chapel under the tower, so I ordered and arranged the altar flowers. Members of the families often spent the night in one of our guest rooms, which meant that we had them for breakfast, for which I was cook. (In order for her not to have too many work hours—and I needed her most for dinner—our maid arrived at noon.)

The secretary of a student organization dropped by to ask if I could give beds to several visiting girl delegates for a religious conference.

A subscriber to the Woolsey Hall concert series was taken suddenly ill, and his wife telephoned to know if on such short notice I could find two boys who would like to use their tickets. This meant quite a lot of telephone calls, but eventual success.

A student came to borrow an ice-bag.

An alumnus many miles and years away from the university dropped by between trains, having made no appointments ahead, and found all the people he hoped to talk with out of town, or in meetings or classes. I filled in until some-one was free.

This is just a small sample of what constantly went on to keep me on the run.

There were calls to be paid on other faculty wives, which ate up a lot of time. Although not as hard and fast a ritual as it formerly was, it still went on to a degree, and a little silver tray stood on the front hall table where calling cards accumulated. Each call had to be returned, soon, and although they were all very short affairs, practically "pop calls," it meant a hat and gloves, and driving here and there in New Haven and the suburbs, which did take time. Only two, or at the most, three calls could be killed off in an afternoon. The wives of any new Branford Fellows would be called on early in the fall, and "welcomed to all the rights and privileges." The poor young things! They probably dreaded a call from me quite as much as I dreaded making it!

Letters from students' mothers, upset about one thing or another, usually came to the college office, but occasionally made up part of my mail. Here is a sample:

I hope if all goes well to come to New Haven for graduation. My question is this: What is the date of gradua-tion? What are any pertinent facts I should know in order to prepare for the trip, etc.? Are there any special social affairs including parents? In fact, any information or suggestions you can give me will be greatly appreciated. I have never been east of the Mississippi before, so you see, it will be a really big experience for me. I am looking forward to all the thrills attendant upon John's graduation from Yale, but I confess am a little uneasy too. What clothes should I bring?

She evidently hadn't read carefully any of the information sent to all parents of graduating seniors about the event, or her son's letters, in which I am sure he at least gave her the date.

WE WERE not supposed to pamper the boys, nor pester them with attention. They had their own lives and friends, and some of them had no need or even desire for our personal friendship, but a large majority saw us as something like a neighbor's family at home, or an aunt and uncle, not too prominent in their lives, but there to be called on if needed.

In looking through student registration cards, I noticed that birth dates were given, and I wondered if sending each a birthday card at the appropriate time would be considered as a little friendly gesture, or too much of "putting in an oar." In a stationary store one day shortly afterward, I ran across some nice-looking birthday cards with none of the "just because you're you," "have a nice day in every way" silly jingles, but a quiet blue and tan border, and only the greeting, "Happy birthday." On impulse, I bought several boxes of them and began sending them to Branford students, simply signing my husband's name and mine. Every one brought back a note of thanks, and from one boy from a broken home came this pathetic line, "You are the only people in the whole world who remembered my birthday."

After the ski season began, weekends meant broken legs and casts, and I was really useful then, for there were always a few of our boys on crutches who needed a ride up the long pull of Prospect Hill to the labs, and then I also had to keep an eye on my watch to be sure to go after them at the right time—too early rather than too late, or they would have begun to try to make it down on their own.

Whenever a boy had a personal problem, and neither the master nor the office secretary was available at the moment, he was apt to come into the house and talk to me instead. At any time, day or night, he might drop in to borrow something or to find the answer to questions such as these:

"Can you recommend a good dentist—and about how much is he apt to charge for a filling?"

"Where can I have a watch repaired?"

"Is there any place in the country nearby where I can go on Sunday afternoon and cut wood for my fireplace? And can you lend me an axe and a saw for this?"

(In a tuxedo, with a tie dangling from his hand), "Will you please tie this danged thing so that the bow goes across instead of straight up and down?"

"May I borrow a small stepladder?" "—an icepick?" "—a large screwdriver?" "—a stout needle that will sew through leather?" "—some brass polish?"

"May I keep my penicillin pills in your icebox?" (Which means he would be in every four hours to take one.)

"May I wait in your living room for a telephone call from my girl? I took the liberty of giving her your number, as the things we have to discuss are rather private, and I have two roommates."

"What would be a good thing to give my mother for her birthday? And will you help me pick it out?"

"Do you have a sewing machine? If so, will you help me make (in other words, will I make) a jester's costume for Saturday night's play?"

"How does one answer an engraved wedding invitation?

Does it mean I have to give a present?" (He isn't going; it is in Oregon.)

"Do you have a road map for the state of Maryland?"

"Do you have a projector that I can borrow to look at the slides I took last weekend?"

They never asked the one question that I would expect: "How can I get to meet some New Haven girls?" Either they were not interested in the species, had already met a satisfactory number during freshman year, or their steady girl back home was all they wanted.

Sometimes the questions were not so easy to answer. "If your grandfather, who was putting you through college, expected you to go into either the ministry or the law, and you would rather die first, and he was beginning to pin you down, how would you break it to the old gentleman?"

I am not a psychiatrist, nor a mother confessor. The things they brought to me were not of world-shattering importance, nor the deepest problems of their souls. But I think it was a very good thing for there to be a *home* near to these boys, belonging to them, in fact, and a woman there their mothers' age, who knew them individually and not just as members of the college, who liked them, and to whom they could talk about anything at all, silly or important.

Here is an example. After a quiet, rather shy sophomore had stayed interminably one afternoon, and talked of everything under the sun without arriving at any point at all—and there was always a point, when they came in—he suddenly blurted out, "It's simply wonderful to talk with you like this! I hope I haven't bored you too much. Do you know, I've been in New Haven almost two years, and you are the first woman I've spoken to who wasn't behind a desk or a counter?"

All sorts of situations arose. One night after a big football game, which we won, and consequently a good deal of celebrating was going on, the phone rang about midnight.

"Could the master come down to police headquarters and identify and vouch for a student who had had a little trouble making a left turn? A hundred dollars for bail should accompany him."

The master happened to be in bed with the flu. I was pinch-hitter, making my first visit to a police station.

Before another football weekend a boy came through from the office, found me in the living room, and asked me politely if I knew how to sew. He didn't want any actual sewing done, he hastened to assure me, but just some practical *sewing advice*—something probably very simple. He and his roommate had girls coming for the weekend, and a party planned, and wanted things to be "really sharp." They decided their room needed a little freshening up. They had gone down and bought some flowered material to cover their couch and make some cushion covers. They had thought making the things would be easy—just straight lines, and the couch cover wouldn't even have to be sewed at all, just thrown over. But when they spread the goods out, it seemed to go off sideways, and although they had measured beforehand very carefully, they were afraid they weren't going to have enough, and—to make a long story short, they simply didn't know how to go about making them. What should they do?

"Have you cut into it?"

Oh no; they had not dared. So far, they had only looked at it. In fact, they didn't have any scissors, and thought they might possibly borrow a pair from me.

I suggested that probably the first thing to do was to draw a thread. He was completely dumbfounded. What was "drawing a thread?" Then he had a brilliant idea. Could they bring the material over and let me *show* them? When I said it was quite simple, but that I'd be glad to demonstrate, he went to the front door and opened it. His roommate, who had been leaning up against it, his arms full of some pretty, gay material, fell headlong into the house. We went up to the sewing room and spread the stuff out and I tried to tell them what to do.

"Now, Mrs. B.," one of the boys said after a few minutes of this. "I think you will admit that we are all busy people. Don't you agree with me that it would save everybody's time if we washed your windows or dusted your books or something, while you made these—things?"

He was a smart boy. So while I sewed, one of them brushed the dog and the other read out loud to us. He was a very smart boy, for the thing he selected to read for our entertainment was his English assignment for the following day.

On another occasion, a senior came in the middle of a morning with, "Can I ask you a very serious question? Mrs. B., (gulp) how much does being married cost?"

I got out the itemized account books that I kept during the first years of our marriage and let him go through them. He was staggered. *"Can opener, $3.75?"* he asked in horror.

He went away, a most dejected young man. Yet not too dejected, because the following June we received an invitation to his wedding.

10

*A*fter we had settled into some sort of routine, I found that I had attained the dignity of what Katherine Mansfield referred to in her journal as "deserving to have a table in one's room," for many hours now found me sitting at that table-desk in a nest of paper and account books and little three-by-five index cards.

Lists, lists, lists! To be made, to be checked off! Fellows of the college, Associate Fellows, former Fellows, wives of them all, widows of former Fellows, sophomores, juniors, seniors, parents of students, alumni. They all had to have some recognition, something done about them, a sandwich or a cup of tea, a cocktail or glass of punch put in their hands, and in order to do it, instead of my former hit-or-miss program of having guests (to my husband: "By the way, isn't it about time *we* had a party?"), I had to be businesslike and alphabetize everybody. No more spontaneous entertaining of personal friends. They didn't even get asked to our house anymore unless they fitted into one of the Branford categories. I was inundated in people to whom I must give food and drink.

Because all this entertaining we had to do was for the university, we had an expense allowance for it, and that meant that accounts had to be kept. "What happened to that ten dollar bill I gave you on Friday?" has never been an easy question for me to answer. I figure that since I try to be as economical and spend as little as possible, what earthly good does it do to write it down? And I never had time before to do it, anyway; I was floundering happily in the business of renovating an old house, and gardening, and taking care of three children.

But now, all had to be written down, and everything had to *balance*, recipes had to be worked out for various numbers, punch ingredients had to be figured for 90, for 140, for 300. How many sandwiches should be made for 35 alumni? For 35 students? (These would be different numbers, since boys don't hold with the tiny bite that a grown-up calls a sandwich.) How many quarts of mayonnaise? How many pounds of salted nuts? All payments for extra party help had to be kept straight. The cost of everything must be presented faultlessly in a little book, all totted up correctly, and with totals ready to be brought out at a minute's notice if called for the inspection by some archangel or other. To a person used to keeping house for only a small private family in rather a slapdash manner, this was an exhausting and testy business, even if the archangel happened to be only one's own husband, grown suddenly very demanding about accuracy. Many an hour which before the move I had looked forward to having free (for playing the piano, for instance), I floundered away at my table-desk, in a perfect labyrinth of columns of ginger ale and waitresses and chocolate cake and percentages. Two lemons for Sunday afternoon tea, when they were 3 for 25 cents, is evidently 2/3 of 25, which is 50/3, which is 16 2/3 cents, call it 17 cents (surely there will be no quibble over a third of a cent). If for a student dinner we have a twenty-pound turkey, and there is enough left over for the family for the next night, and sandwiches for lunch the following day, exactly how much of that turkey's original cost should Mother Yale pay for, as college entertaining, and how much come from Father Buck's pocket as food for his family?

OF ALL the people listed on my three-by-five cards, the students were the first to be taken care of. We wanted each one, during the time he lived in Branford, to come for dinner and an evening with us. After they came by invitation and found the way, and learned that we were always at home Sunday afternoons at tea time, they could drop in on us then or not, just as they chose. And while some didn't so choose, many of them did.

Our dining table seated fourteen, so with my husband at one end and me at the other, we could have twelve boys at a time. We took them in groups of roommates, for while it was good for them to meet in our house and mingle with boys they did not know as well, conversation was easier at first if at least a few close friends were there together.

Yale boys come from every class of society, and any entertaining of groups of twelve, chosen at random, had to be done carefully. One of them might live perhaps on New York's Park Avenue, or its equivalent in some other city, fly to Paris or Palm Beach for weekends with his parents in their second homes, while the boy sitting next to him might come from Cross Corners in the Ozarks, might have been milking six cows every day since he was twelve years old, and did not even possess a second suit. The wife of one of the masters, herself a Park Avenue product, once wore an evening gown that was practically backless at a student dinner at their home in the college and some of her unsophisticated guests, who had never seen such a dress before except in the movies, were so thoroughly intimidated that they never dared again set foot in their master's house or approach him in any way.

I learned by sad experience all the tricks that have to be resorted to in sending out dinner invitations to students. To begin with, when we asked twelve, we couldn't expect that all of the first asked could come. They were so enmeshed in the myriad activities of student life that finding a free evening wasn't easy. One would have a debate, one would be rehearsing for a "dramat" play. Glee club rehearsals took two stated evenings a week, fraternities another; there were lectures and concerts, tests the next day, and whatnot. Tests could be scheduled at any time at all. A mere dinner invitation had to take a back seat. I always had at least three alternates to whom I could pop off invitations if regrets came in.

In the second place, any invitation, unless we wanted to get into a perfectly fearful mixup which might result in twenty boys showing up or only two, had to be in writing, and put in the mailbox in Yale station *exactly five days ahead*, no more, no less. If it were sent only three days early, he might not get it, because if his girl wasn't writing to him now, he might not go for his mail more than twice a week. Whereas if we asked him as much as eight days ahead, he might show up the day after he received the invitation, and not on the Wednesday following for which he was asked. If we asked him too soon, he might forget all about it before the time came; if we asked him too late, he already had another engagement. Five days ahead was the perfect time.

A third danger: students paid no heed to the initials R.S.V.P. The whole thing had to be written out ("Please let the office secretary know before noon Monday whether or not we may expect you"). They couldn't miss that, and most of them would let her know. Almost every student room had a telephone, so around four o'clock on Monday afternoon, if there was anyone who hadn't reported to the secretary, I would try to reach him by phone.

"Oh, sure, I'm coming. I asked my roommate to let you know; didn't he do it?"

"Gosh, I forgot all about letting you know. I am planning to come if I haven't gummed things up."

On one occasion, after I failed to reach someone who had not answered, I got a note on the next day from a very contrite and humiliated boy. He said he was quite absentminded, so printed signs to himself and put them all around his room to remind him of things. He had made one about our dinner and stuck it on the outside of his door, so that the minute he got in from the library that afternoon he could change and be ready. But just as he was leaving the library the boy he had been studying with said, "Come along to Davenport with me to dinner, why don't you? Then we can keep on with this after dinner." It was only after he got back to his own room about ten that he read his sign.

Another boy told us he was so banged up at football practice that by the time they finished putting adhesive and raw beefsteak on him he decided he looked too frightening to appear.

Every Wednesday night, we had one of these dinners for seniors, gradually working our way down the class list. I didn't try any fancy menu, but just something like a regular family turkey dinner, ending with several kinds of ice cream. A different batch of boys was there each week to eat it, and by having exactly the same thing for the same number, preparation and serving were made as easy as possible. We knew exactly how many pounds of sweet potatoes to peel, how many extra quarts of milk to order. So as to have everything ready, I kept the china, silver, and glasses we used for them in a special cupboard, counted out in fourteens; I laundered and ironed the big damask dinner napkins the day after every dinner, and set the table myself on Wednesday morning. An extra maid—two if I could get them—came in to help serve, and there was always a cook in the kitchen.

On one unforgettable Wednesday, not hearing any bustling around noise but only abysmal silence in the kitchen, I investigated about three o'clock and found, instead of a busy cook, a note from her on the counter: "I am taking a job at Winchesters factory. Sorry to leave this good place and you been good to me but they pay more. Love. Edna." Twelve hungry boys were coming at six-thirty; there wasn't even time to be angry. I really turned around fast. The extra maid who usually came to serve arrived on time, was not a bit upset by having to take on the whole table alone, and said calmly that she had been expecting this, for Edna had been trying out at various factories on her days off for some time.

Dinner was only a little late, and when I explained what had happened it broke any ice there might have been, and many of the boys then contributed hilarious accounts of times in their homes when their mothers had been caught in like or even worse situations.

When it was time to remove the plates, I had every other boy take out his and the one on his right, set them on the long table in the butler's pantry, and bring back the dessert plates already filled by the maid and waiting on the counter. The boys rather enjoyed seeing what was behind the scenes in the kitchen.

There were only a few "incidents" at these senior dinners. Once a phone call to the room of a boy who had accepted but failed to show up brought no answer. We waited half an hour, then decided he had forgotten all about it, and started without him, risking thirteen at the table and the calamity it is supposed to bring. Halfway through the meal he appeared, breathless and embarrassed, slid into the vacant chair, and stammered out his apologies. He had been at the chem lab until four, then was signed up to give blood at the Red Cross blood drive. There was a bottleneck there, and he had to wait two hours before they got to him. When he was finally finished with, he didn't even wait for the half-hour lie-down that donors are supposed to take, and the sandwich and brandy or coffee or whatever it is they give them, but got right up from the cot and ran all the way here. Just as he finished telling us all this he fainted.

Finger bowls confounded a few. Occasionally a boy would tell me later that it was at our table that he was faced for the first time with the horrendous problem of what to do with one. One boy, who was evidently having his first encounter with a finger bowl, caught on by watching his neighbor that it should be lifted off to the left, so that the dessert that the maid was bringing around could be helped onto the plate underneath, but he failed to see, and so left behind, the little lace mat under the finger bowl. He gave himself a generous helping of ice cream, right on top of the mat, and in a few minutes was embarrassingly entangled in a mouthful of both.

Sometimes table conversation was a little stilted at first, and to get things under way Steve and I would drag out the same old stories we had often heard each other tell. But it didn't matter, for it was always a different group of listeners, and although we had heard them before, the boys hadn't. Soon this priming of the pump worked, and they were coming up with adventures and experiences of their own. Long before we returned to the living room for coffee, everything was moving smoothly.

For the evening's entertainment, we set up the screen and showed them a Yale movie. In the fall, it would be the preceding Saturday's football game, in which they were always interested, for it might have been an out-of-town game that they hadn't seen, or if played here perhaps they hadn't gone, or had poor seats, or there could have been disputed calls that they wanted to see again. To show at alumni gatherings and to prospective students, the university had made a film called "Life in an Undergraduate College at Yale," with many of the scenes shot in Branford, with Branford students taking part. We had a copy of it, and when football was not in season, we showed this film. The boys delighted in seeing themselves and hooting at their fellow actors. During the Advent season, Steve played the piano for them, and we wound up the evening with Christmas carols.

These student dinners took up much more time than the actual Wednesday evenings and getting the table ready. My husband knew most of the seniors well already; he had taught many in a required Economics course, he talked with them about their grades, their finances if there was trouble; he assigned their rooms in the fall, knew who their roommates were and straightened out things if there was any trouble there; he had all their records in his office, and had worked with them constantly on college projects. He ate lunch in their dining hall practically every day, and often at a table of both Fellows and students.

I had none of this working contact with the boys. I only saw them passing beneath the windows on the way to classes or meals; my only chance to chat had been with the ones who dropped around on Sunday afternoons for tea or during the week with a question or request for something, so I had to learn about them from their pictures and the information on their cards in the office files.

On the days preceding a dinner I would spend many evening hours in the college office, poring over the folders of the boys who were next on the dinner list, trying to assimilate all the information there. I had taken my first shot at these cards when they were entering as Branford sophomores, but kept going back over them whenever I knew I would be encountering certain ones. Everything was there, beginning with his picture, full name, and the name by which he was called. Having this last was quite an aid, for as in the White Knight's poem in *Alice*, "the name of the song" and "the name the song is called by" were sometimes two different things. James Charles Smith might just as likely be called Chuck as Jim. Sometimes you were presented with something like Bobo, Whizzer, or Moose; and while this was all very well for fellow students, it did not seem quite the thing for a master's wife to greet a perfectly strange boy with "Hello, Stinky."

There was also on each student's card his father's college if any, and occupation, other family members, where prepared for Yale, standing in class, major interests, hobbies, college major, etc. Before our twelve guests arrived, I felt I could recognize each one, knew them pretty well, and was primed enough with talking points to start things off at least. One of the delights of the evening for me was the astonishment on the boys' faces when they came in, and I could greet each one by name, although we might not have met before. I never confessed to the dogged hours I had spent over their cards.

Every now and then I played a trick on them. I would pick out perhaps two of the boys who were coming, and learn their draft numbers. Then when the subject of my knowing all their names came up—and it always did—I would say casually, "I've got a pretty good memory for things like that. For instance—" picking out a boy supposedly at random—"Tom's draft number is such-and-such." This was met with utter amazement by them all, especially Tom. "What's mine?" "What's mine?" several more would immediately clamor. If the other one whose number I had learned asked, I gave it—otherwise I would say, "Of course I can't pretend to know all of them, but"—selecting the one I had learned— "Sam's is———," and I would give it. "Now don't let's talk about draft numbers anymore; I only hope they never have to be used." Alas, during 1942–45, they did.

Besides the Wednesday dinners for fourteen, and Sunday afternoon teas for "whosoever will," one evening a week at nine we had the lower-classmen in in groups of twenty for cider and doughnuts, cookies and Coke, to sit around on the floor and chat or sing Yale songs around the piano. Sometimes there was a boy in the group who was glad to get his hands on a Steinway; if not, Steve would play the accompaniment. We kept on hand quite a stack of the little grey Yale song books, which contain all the college glees for several generations back—"Let Bacchus to Venus libations pour fast," " 'Twas Friday night when we set sail," "There is a tavern in the town," etc., and college songs known and loved in those days on every campus, like "Far Above Cayuga's Waters," and "Gaudeamus Igitur." There were present-day college songs, of course, football songs, those from the world wars, like "It's a long way to Tipperary," "Over There," and "There's a long, long trail"—which incidentally was written by a Yale man, a classmate of my husband's. The boys whose voices were not good enough to get them into any of the university singing organizations, but who like to sing, especially enjoyed these evenings.

There were big parties to be given throughout the year on specific dates, like the annual Christmas party for the Fellows and their wives, held in the college dining hall, but with drinks at our house first; and parents' weekend in the fall, when a couple of hundred of them would show up; and of course at graduation for the seniors and their families.

Whenever there was a crowd I would engage one of the team of caterers, bartenders, and extra maids who went from house to house at these parties, and knew every Yale kitchen and pantry down to the last fork and glass. Thurlow Jones was the prince of bartenders, sure to be in charge of some Yale party every weekend. Jennie Flynn, a brisk young Irishwoman, had organized a group of her friends and relatives into efficient teams who would prepare party food in their homes and walk in bearing great trays of delectable cold things, and things on baking sheets ready to be slipped into the oven. The only snag was that you had to scramble for these wonderful people, and be sure you signed them up before some other Yale hostess snagged them.

Parties for families and parents were more fun than any of the others, and the graduation parties, at which we were all very emotional, were the best of all. Here roommates' families met each other often for the first time; faraway mothers were thanking nearby mothers who had taken care of their sons on holidays, prep school brothers were looking the place over and meeting other students' brothers who might be their roommates later if they succeeded in getting into Yale, pretty sisters were meeting their brothers' roommates they had heard about (and perhaps dreamed about), small brothers and sisters were bent upon trying the champagne punch instead of the fruit juice punch which had been provided especially for them.

The confusion of modern family life sometimes made for tense situations in the receiving line. A student's family might consist of a divorced mother and her second husband, who did not speak to the father and his second wife and their child. All would be acting very possessive, including his adoring grandmother who had raised him and who was glaring at them all, and his little fiancée, trembling at this formidable array of relatives she was taking on.

There was a problem of *names,* too, in such cases, for presupposing—correctly usually, but not always—that we knew *his* name, a boy was quite apt to present his parents at these receptions with the unhelpful statement, "This is my mother," or, "This is my stepfather." In the crush and expedition of the receiving line, even a perfectly well-known name might not always immediately rise to one's tongue, and when it was necessary to turn immediately and introduce these parents to the next in line, recourse to polite muttering was sometimes the only solution.

The night before one of these parties was another time when I would apply myself studiously to the records to try to straighten out all the information we had about the family. A Yale father who worked his heart out on alumni committees would not appreciate being asked chattily whether this was his first visit to New Haven.

Occasionally some student had a famous literary or political father, or a well-known mother. Once one of our students claimed a princess as his mother! Also occasionally there were rural relatives by whom the boy was embarrassed, and was also ashamed of being embarrassed.

One little second-generation Italian mother refused to move on down the receiving line in spite of her graduate son's desperate prodding. She tucked in beside me and stayed there, and she would not budge in spite of all he could do. She was a darling little bright-eyed person, and we constantly exchanged smiles.

Then she ruined it all as she chirped, looking up into my face with a twinkle, "Do you know why I like you? It's because you're so plain!"

II

"O day of rest and gladness!" Rest? On Sunday? I was the proverbial dishrag when it was over, but usually a very happy, contented dishrag.

We always began Sunday by setting a good example. The college chapel was just across the street, and our family was always there en masse. As dean of the freshmen, Steve had to wear his blue academic robe, march in the procession behind the choir, and sit in one of the seats of the mighty on the platform, along with the university president, the college chaplain, the preacher of the morning, and one or two other members of the administration who spelled each other at the job. I herded the children into a pew near the front, and we settled ourselves for a pious hour.

The children were entranced with the whole service. A Branford boy they knew sang in the choir, and he winked at the little girls as the choir passed our pew. They were delighted with the building itself. "People sit around up under the roof!" they said.

Almost every Sunday there was a different preacher, and occasionally a member of our family livened up the hour a bit. One morning Secunda dropped her collection quarter, and upset a number of people as she pursued it under a couple of pews as it rolled away; then there was the first time I thought, mistakenly as it turned out, that Tercia was old enough to attend. For some time she had been wild to go with the others to see that remarkable sight of people sitting around under the roof, and had pleaded with me so piteously, and crossed her heart and hoped to die if she made any noise or a single word escaped her, that weakly I gave in.

She was properly impressed and excited by the great event of being allowed to go to Battell with the rest of the family, and having told her for about the twentieth time that there must be *no conversation,* no matter what happened that she wanted to comment on, I gave my last instruction just before we entered.

"Now, Tercia, the first thing each person does inside is to kneel, close her eyes, and make a short little prayer."

She knew what a prayer was, all right, having said one at my knee every night of her life, so as soon as she was in the pew, she knelt obediently, and with tightly squinched-up eyes, and a voice, audible if not at Heaven's gates themselves then at least to five pews in every direction, prayed earnestly, "O God, help me to keep quiet in church!"

The most memorable brightening of the morning service by a member of our family, however, was not anything the children did, but a lapse on my husband's part.

There was a very eloquent preacher that morning, who held the entire congregation, including my husband, spellbound. Steve was so mesmerized by the preacher's words, so completely unaware of his surroundings in fact, that he did the thing that he constantly did unconsciously when concentrating on anything: reached for a cigarette. To my dismay, I saw him reach inside his robe and take out a packet of

Camels, extract one, tap it down on the arm of the pontifical chair in which he sat, and return the packet. Then, horror of horrors, still as transfixed as a sleepwalker, he began to slap his pockets in search of his lighter. Why I didn't die on the spot, I'll never know. He was in plain sight of the whole chapel full of students and faculty, many of whom had noticed what he was about, and had withdrawn their attention from the minister to watch with fiendish expectation this much more entrancing sideshow of a lighter about to flare in the sanctuary. Never, even when I was trying to prevent the celestial delivery from on high of a pony, have I prayed as earnestly as I did then. "Oh, Steve, come to! For heavens' sake, come to! Remember where you are! *Don't* flick that lighter!" I must have been living right, for my prayer was answered. With only a fraction of a second before he would have been eternally disgraced, he did come to, but the story of what almost happened is still remembered and talked about at Yale.

Meanwhile, over at our house every Sunday morning the cook, whose church fortunately held its services at night, would be busily baking cookies and making sandwiches for the imminent student tea party. In order not to interrupt her we went over to the college dining hall for our noon dinner.

Every Sunday afternoon all year was given to our tea party for whoever wished to come. It meant, of course, that we had to give up our own private family life at that time. There were plenty of Sundays when we would rather have been doing something else, like a walk in the woods, or a ride through the country to see the October color, a visit to friends in a nearby town, or just a good plain long sleep. But we were here to take care of the student needs and not primarily our own wants. To tell them that we would be at home every third Sunday, or the first one in every month, would have registered with them about as clearly as expecting them to figure out for themselves when Easter would come—something like high tide after the second full moon in April, or some such rigmarole. They would never have kept such dates straight, nor would we. It had to be *every Sunday*, or none. So every Sunday it was.

The result was that our children were Sunday orphans. But they didn't care; they loved being orphans. The mother-in-law of the office secretary, a darling old lady whom the children adored and to whose visits they looked forward, came for the afternoon. They called her "Granny," and I am afraid wound her around their nimble little fingers.

With the children thus disposed of, I sat at the tea table in the living room in front of one of the fireplaces, with cheerful fires on cold afternoons, and as I poured cups of really good Chinese tea, got a chance to chat a bit with each boy. They always came back for seconds, and often for thirds. The platters of sandwiches and cookies kept passing around and being emptied and refilled, and on the dining room table was a stack of dessert plates and forks and three large layer cakes, presided over by no one. During the course of the afternoon, the boys meandered in and cut their own— as large a slice or as many as they chose (and who's counting?). I had a standing order at the Swiss bakery for those twelve-inch cakes with different frostings—always a chocolate; it went first but all three disappeared completely before tea was done.

Although "tea in a faculty home" is a stock subject for ridicule by campus cartoonists the world over, we had from thirty to fifty-five boys every Sunday. Many of them turned up every week. These teas were a godsend to boys whose dates didn't know enough to go home and were still hanging around Sunday afternoon. Occasionally there were visiting parents to do something with, and what better than to introduce them to the college master? Bachelor Fellows were steady customers, often we had a married one with his wife. A boy giving a weekend to heavy studying would welcome a break in the middle of the afternoon. A lonely, homesick boy was happy to get into a family atmosphere, gregarious boys to have a whole gang to talk with, and always, boys of any age who liked to eat were happy to have the opportunity. For a boy who wasn't an easy conversationalist, there were spread around a number of cartoon books—collections from *New Yorker* people like Peter Arno, Helen Hokinson, Chan Day, George Hill—and often some student would ensconce himself at the end of a sofa and spend the entire afternoon chuckling his way through them, and honestly tell me when he left—although he may not have spoken twenty words the whole time—that he had had a wonderful afternoon. Lying around on the small tables were also a few of those geometric wooden or plastic puzzles to work out, such as the well-known "mystic star" that fell to pieces if you touched it and that was the very dickens to fit together again, and somebody was always working on them or giving suggestions to the manipulator.

There was no way that I ever found to predict how many boys might show up. Three is the least number we ever had, and that was during a spring vacation when everybody was out of town. After one of the big football games, we were surprised to have only eight. Everybody must have been exhausted and was sleeping, or had to prepare Monday's assignments, neglected so far in all the hoopla of the weekend. On the next big game weekend I expected our tea-drinkers to follow the same pattern; we had sixty. A beautiful weekend when I figured they'd all be playing tennis or taking sunbaths, they came to tea. Other pretty weekends they played tennis or took sunbaths, and the family ate stale sandwiches and cake the rest of the week. On chill, gloomy days, just made for a cup of tea before an open fire, they slept. Or else dozens of them came trooping in for tea. There was no earthly way to foretell which it would be, or at least if there was I never found it out. On one never-to-be-forgotten day we had seventy-two. The food gave out early, of course; the cook worked frantically all afternoon making more sandwiches, and a couple of the boys went back and helped her. Before it was over we had even opened boxes of Wheat Thins and Ritz crackers and raided the children's supply of Fig Newtons. The last twenty-five to come didn't even know that earlier in the afternoon there had been three huge cakes.

The boys could get plenty of cocktails in their own rooms and in those of their peers, for there were numerous small student parties on Sunday afternoons where more powerful drinks than tea flowed freely. But for those among the three hundred or so in our charge, for "whosoever wants to come" there was a welcome in the master's house with food, hot tea, and good talk, and a homelike atmosphere they wouldn't get elsewhere, sometimes not even in their own homes. I didn't fool myself into thinking that food didn't play a large part in bringing the boys, but a leaping fire on a winter Sunday afternoon, and lively conversation with the master and with each other, was the real drawing card.

12

It was an all-male Yale while we lived in Branford, but on weekends, especially football weekends, girls from nearby New England colleges flooded the place. The railroad station was a mass of excited young Yale boys eagerly scanning the line stepping off the train to pick out their dates. Any girls who had cars, or could pick up rides with those who did, came that way, so all the available parking places anywhere near the university were soon filled. Narrow little High Street was jammed with cars half off and half on the sidewalk and street, with parking tickets stuck behind many a windshield wiper. With our own car tucked snugly in its garage right there within a stone's throw, where it could stay indefinitely, my heart went out to those out-of-towners limited to one hour. An hour's parking was no time at all. I often did my good deed for the day by taking out a handful of dimes and walking all the way up the block, putting them in the slots of parking meters whose time had already run out, or was just about to do so. I was caught at it once by the metermaid, who was writing out tickets with relish, and she was furious with me.

The Hotel Taft provided rooms for most of the girls, but the guest facilities at the college masters' houses were always filled, too. The other masters' houses had rooms for more girls than we did. Some even had dormitory space where they could take care of a number—twenty-seven at Silliman, twenty-one at Berkeley. The girls didn't mind being crowded, since they spent very little time in the rooms, anyway.

We had only two rooms we could use for them, which meant only four girls could stay with us, and the boys spoke for those rooms far in advance. But occasionally a couple in distress would ring our doorbell on Saturday with a pitiful tale. There had been a mixup, and a boy who thought he had a room reserved at the Taft found a girl on his hands with no place to put her. Or she might have said at first that she couldn't come, then changed her mind and with no warning, arrived. On a stormy night, a boy who was to have put his girl up with friends in Cheshire or Woodbridge would find the roads glare ice and couldn't make it out there.

In emergencies I would double up my own children, clear their bathroom of turtles or whatever other animal was in residence at the time, and take in an extra girl or two. But this was never too good an idea, for it brought her into the family end of the hall. A child might suddenly get sick in the night—their favorite time for doing it—the visitor might come in very late and wake us all up by bumbling around feeling for light switches, or she might want to sleep late the next morning while the dispossessed daughter determinedly insisted that she simply had to get something out of *her own room*. Or some other complication might arise.

The children were violently against being turned out of their beds, too. They adored the college boys, but perhaps from jealousy, even at their early ages, they bore no love for the visiting girls.

(Traveling in England years later, Tercia arrived in London one night with no hotel reservation, and after several calls to hotels she knew failed to secure one. She then brazenly called up one of our former students, then living in London, and asked if he and his wife could put her up for the night.

(I was horrified when she told me about it. "They owed me," she said calmly. "I gave up my room one whole weekend so his girl could have it. I remember perfectly well."

("But you don't remember 'perfectly well,'" I wailed, "He didn't marry that girl; your London hostess was a different person entirely!")

I did nothing about meals for these visiting girls; the boys who were their hosts fed them, usually in the college dining hall; we only slept them. I turned over a key to the front door to the boy, and then they were on their own. I used to give the key to the girl, but she could never find it again in the conglomeration of her purse's contents, or else would lose it some other way, so that the lock therefore had to be changed. So I learned to give the key to the boy and watch while he snapped it on his keyring. I could always get it from him later if he neglected to return it at the end of the weekend.

Our house rule was "goodnight at the door"; no one sat up for these girls, or checked on what time they got in. I left a list on the front hall table; they scratched their names off as they came in, and the last one in put the chain on the door and turned off the lights. If anyone wanted to be waked at any special time, such as to go to early church, she left a note informing me as to which room and which bed she was occupying, so I wouldn't risk rousing the wrong girl, which I did a time or two.

These visiting girls were my worst headaches. Sometimes the boys found them that, too, such as one who was to have been ready for breakfast at ten and church at eleven, and was not on time for either, as she made an elaborate toilet. I could understand why these young women were all so pretty: they spent time on it!

One boy was marching up and down the living room, watch in hand, one Sunday noon. "If she doesn't come down within the next five minutes," he said, "and she won't, that will make an even two hours that I have spent waiting for her this weekend."

The authorities at the colleges the girls attended were apparently glad to have them off their campuses for the weekend, but mothers and prep school headmistresses hovered over their younger ones, calling me on the phone and writing me notes to urge me to watch over their little darlings. I refused categorically, saying they were welcome as our house guests, but that I would take no responsibility as chaperone. If a girl were not mature enough to manage a weekend at a male college, she shouldn't come.

Most of the girls would arrive Saturday around noon, since they, as well as the boys, often had early Saturday classes. A few always came in on Friday, however, and of those few, a few instead of sleeping late on Saturday morning as any right-minded girl would do if she had the chance, would rise bright and early, come down looking around for some breakfast, and then dog my steps around the house until her date was free at twelve. On Saturday mornings, especially football Saturdays when my husband always felt we were hopelessly late if we did not get to the Bowl not only in time for the kickoff but to see the warm-ups as well, I was frantically busy, with no free time to date-sit.

Once a boy came by on Friday to pick up the key, telling me that his girl would be arriving "early Saturday morning." About 2:00 A.M. I was awakened by the unmistakable sounds of someone's breaking into the house; the burglar that I had been expecting for years had finally arrived. Feeling like Blondie Bumstead, who is always sending poor Dagwood down in the middle of the night to confront burglars, I waked Steve, and with my heart in my throat watched him stumble down the stairs. What if they were armed? When he turned on the living room light, there must have been quite a tableau. In the doorway, a rumpled, half-awake master, barefooted and in pajamas. In the middle of the living room floor, a suitcase. A student stood at an open window, helping a girl, half in and half out, climb through it.

When the light flashed on, she gave a feeble little yelp, and fell the rest of the way into the room. The boy caught her, and then, instead of being abashed for entering the house so unceremoniously, turned to Steve reproachfully. "I *told* your wife that Nancy would get here *early Saturday*, but the front door had the chain on!"

If a boy found that he lacked something, he simply did without, but a girl would come trotting helplessly to me: "Would you mind?" The things they forgot to bring, and expected me to provide!

They always arrived bareheaded, and then if they learned that their dates wanted to go to the Sunday morning chapel service, where hats on females were then *de rigeur,* they borrowed mine. There were occasions when every hat I owned was worshiping in Battell Chapel on Sunday morning.

When they took rumpled dresses out of their bags, they came to me to get them pressed. I couldn't ask the cook to do this, for she had plenty of her own work. The girls would flutter helplessly around in the servants' dining room where we kept the ironing board set up, and usually I found myself doing the pressing myself. A needle and thread was often in requisition too. And who was plying it? Right.

And the telephoning they did! If my husband in his office across the street wanted to tell me something, it was quicker for him to walk across the street and say it than to wait until the phone was free. They kept it tied up with calls to people they knew in New Haven—often to other boys. (This was known as "bird-dogging": coming down on one boy's invitation and hoping to transfer to another and more desirable boy after they got here.) Toll calls would often appear on our bill to places where we knew no one. Sometimes there were quarters left by the phone, more often there were not.

They spilled boxes of face powder on the rugs. They got lipstick on my bed linen and face towels. One girl took a torrential, rushing shower at 2:00 A.M. while singing in a deep contralto, "Praise the Lord, and pass the ammunition!"

And the things they forgot and left behind in their own college rooms when they came were nothing to what they left here when they departed, and that I then had to find boxes to fit and take to the post office to mail. Often it was cosmetics, but I always took a look under the beds on Monday morning to see which ones had left bedroom slippers out of sight. After one junior prom, as two girls were leaving they informed me that they had left on one of the beds two huge boxes with their crinolines, to be mailed to them: "Would you mind?" On the trip down to New Haven there had been only two of them in the car and there was room for the dresses, but going back two more girls would be riding with them, so the dresses would have to come by mail. At least they had provided the enormous boxes required. I remember one who didn't.

She wore a cunning little Peter Pan hat when she arrived, with a long feather to her shoulder. When she left she tied a scarf around her hair, and wrote me later to send the hat. (She wrote, of course, "Would you mind?") The feather was not only long, it was stiff and refused to curl; I was faced with the same problem as crating a baby giraffe. I had to go out to a florist and get a box designed for long-stemmed flowers to mail it.

I kept telling myself that perhaps when my three little girls grew up to college age, they would act in the same way.

But in the meantime, give me college *boys* every time.

13

Branford also had a suite of guest rooms on the third floor, not connected with the rest of the house, and entered from the court. This was definitely not for the dates of students, but for the great or near-great guests of the university. If the honorary degree candidates at commencement, for example, were more numerous than the president's house could accommodate, two of them might be sent to us. Sometimes they were foreigners, and at first I used to worry for fear that I would say or do the wrong thing and give the university, or perhaps even America, a black eye, even start a spot of international trouble—a ridiculous idea, of course, for college masters were never entrusted with too important or "combustible" people. If there was a language difference, it was never a problem, although with a Britisher I sometimes wondered if I even understood English. People from abroad were never as provincial as Americans; most of us are apt to speak only our own tongue, but English was sure to be number one of the several languages in which all foreigners were proficient.

Steve taught for three years at the American University in Beirut, and learned a little of his students' native speech while he was there, which I thought might be useful once when we learned that our seats for a football game were next to that of the king of Jordan, who was a guest at the president's house. But it turned out that Hussein had been educated in England, and even understood football, since he had played there on a rugby team.

The men who stayed in the guest suite were here for a particular occasion, to give a lecture, or to learn about some experiment or project that was being carried on at Yale, or to talk with some particular person—at any rate, not to see *us*, so we respected that. They were usually busy every minute inspecting whatever it was they came to see, or consulting with their counterparts on our faculty, but they sometimes brought along a wife who was bored with it all, and while her husband was busy, I tried to be on hand to take care of her.

It was rather fun to see what the great looked like at close quarters; the men were usually interesting, but their wives sometimes were not. The men were up and out early, utilizing every minute about whatever it was they came for, but if the wife was brought along "just for the ride," she was apt to sleep late and come down for breakfast an hour or two later. That meant that breakfast had to be a moveable feast, served whenever there was anybody to eat it. Such a sliding scale would never fit in with any created cook's temper, so in order to keep her cheerful—in fact, in order to keep her at all—I had her go on about her regular work schedule, while I kept an eye and an ear out for the descending guest. I had to spring to action then, as I was generally the breakfast cook.

On one occasion, Steve unwittingly was. A West Point bigwig, here to discuss the ROTC situation with him, was staying with us. As he went upstairs to bed the night before, I said, "We have no set breakfast hour. Come down whenever you wake and are ready for it—eight, nine, ten . . ."

His face fell. My bright husband stepped into the breach. "Or seven or six or five."

"Do you mean that?" Bigwig asked eagerly. "I am afraid that I am an early riser."

My husband was another one. He came down in a bathrobe and made himself a pot of coffee each morning about the time that country roosters begin crowing for day, and long before any hired cook would dream of waking.

The next morning at 4:30 the West Pointer came tipping down the stairs in bedroom slippers and wearing a raincoat over his pajamas. He tentatively pushed open the kitchen door, hoping to find the fixings for coffee, and ran instead into a hard-at-work master seated at the kitchen table surrounded with paperwork, a pot of coffee and a plate of doughnuts at his side.

They greeted each other warmly, for early risers always feel like blood brothers—the only ones wise enough to be awake in an otherwise sluggish world. Another cup was brought, another pot was brewed, and before it was empty the two men had completed all the planning they had expected would take them most of the morning. The visitor sheepishly explained his attire.

"Don't think I was expecting rain in your kitchen, but on a trip I always save space by carrying a raincoat over my arm instead of filling a bag with a bathrobe. Serves the same purpose, and I often need it for rain before I get home, anyway."

Then there was a British woman, the wife of a professor

from the London School of Economics. Utterly uninterested in what brought her husband here, she was enduring her first trip to "the States," and seeing what life was like in the provinces. When she finally appeared on the scene that morning I had had my own breakfast hours before, so I could concentrate on serving hers piping hot. She said that toast and tea was all she was accustomed to eating. There was an electric toaster on the table, and I made one slice after another for her.

Did she eat them? She did not. As slices came from the toaster she upended them at the edge of her plate and sipped her tea, but took no bite. Such beautifully browned toast! I was hungry myself by that time, and looked longingly at the neglected, rapidly cooling slices. I kept plying her with fresh pieces, and finally hinted, "Oh dear, I am afraid your toast is getting quite cold."

"I certainly hope so," she replied bluntly. "That is the idea. My deah, did you never hear of toast racks?"

No, I never had. Patiently she explained them to an American aborigine. You stand warm toast up in them to allow it to get cold and hard as a rock. Only then is it ready to eat.

14

Because the two colleges of Branford and Saybrook were made out of the already existing Harkness Quadrangle, they are as alike as Tweedledum and Tweedledee. With no break in the masonry they stand cheek by jowl on High Street, front and service doors practically identical, so that it was only to be expected that there would be a good deal of confusion as to which was which. Guests, deliveries, and even some service bureau men, who certainly should have known better since they were called to both colleges constantly, often went to the wrong one. Their city street numbers, 80 and 90 High, were much alike too, and to add to the confusion, not far away there were two large apartment buildings numbered 80 and 90 Howe Street. Packages for one came to the other, and vice versa, and guests unfamiliar with New Haven were often left on Howe Street by taxi-drivers and confronted with a choice of fifty push-buttons of unknown names. If one walked down High Street, in broad daylight, and examined every entrance until one came to a number, 80 or 90, in plain sight, with the name of the college on a brass plate there too, it should have been easy to find the right place, but apparently it often wasn't. The darkness of night could complicate things, too.

The front and back doors of the same college were often mistaken for each other; many a guest made his first entrance into our house through the kitchen. Before one of the proms a very elegant undergraduate in tails brought his equally elegant parents to call, via the back door.

Deliveries coming down High Street from the direction of Chapel got to the front door first, and often got no farther. Dry cleaning, fish, racks of Coca-Colas were constantly being left at the front door.

One rainy football Saturday, when the street was jammed with hooting, tooting, impatient, snarling traffic, a student's father, an army officer spangled with stars and gold braid, was saying goodbye at our front door when a delivery boy popped out of a grocery truck, dashed up the front steps, and with a "Here, take it! I'm holding up traffic and that cop'll get me!" thrust into the hands of the great man a white, clammy turkey, its rain- and blood-soaked paper wrapping dropping off it.

Another out-of-the-way front door delivery was a birthday present for me. My husband and I had a pleasant family custom on those days of giving each other what we wanted ourselves, not necessarily what the recipient wanted. Gifts were often things for our Vermont summer home. One year, for example, I gave him a load of well-rotted cow manure for the perennial flower bed, and that same year, for my birthday, he found at a farm auction a side-delivery rake—something I had never seen before, but he had kept talking about wanting as a great help with mowing the fields, as indeed it proved to be.

On this particular birthday morning, when, as it happened, a reception for parents was to be held in the house that afternoon, I answered the front bell to be greeted by an expressman with, "I have a delivery for you. Where shall I leave it? It's pretty big."

I had long ago given up trying to get drivers to move a truck to the back door, once they had parked it in front. Also at that moment the back doorbell rang, so, "Just bring it on in here," I said, "and I'll decide what to do with it later. I have to answer the back door now."

The back door delivery was the grocery order, and there were things to be put away. When I returned to the front of the house, what to my wondering eyes should appear but the knocked-down parts—including the wheels, of course—of a camp trailer, one of those light, four-wheeled things to hang on behind a car. I didn't recognize it as a camp trailer, never having seen one in this dishabille condition before, but I knew at once what it *had to be*—my birthday present from a loving husband, who had yearned for one for years.

But the reception! That very afternoon! The vision of a hundred parents arriving in a few hours to wind their way around the trailer's neatly stacked parts flashed through my mind. I made a sputtering report to my husband, in his freshman office across the street, about what was taking up our front hall.

He was delighted. "Fine business," he positively chortled. "Right on the dot. What does it look like? Don't let the man go until I get there; I am coming right over."

During the few minutes that it took him to cross the street, the expressman cleared up the mystery of why it had been delivered to the house when that was not the address on the tag. It was supposed to have been left at the Athletic Association's garage out on Derby Avenue, where Steve,

who always planned for every contingency, had made ar-
rangements to leave it until we went to the country at term's
end. But no one had told the man in charge out there about
the arrangement, and when he saw the dean's name on the
tag, he simply rerouted it to our home address, thinking he
was saving everybody a lot of trouble. After a blissful strok-
ing, poking, and looking it over generally, Steve reluctantly
sent it back out Derby Avenue; the parents' reception took
place as planned.

Other masters' houses besides Branford and Saybrook
were not always easy to find either. The stone buildings of
which they formed a part were so enormous that a stranger
did not think of a family's living there.

Next to us, on the other side, was Jonathan Edwards
College, and its master's house, number 70 High Street, was
the most difficult of all for a stranger to locate, for its door
opened not on High Street at all but around the corner on
what used to be Library Street. When all the new colleges
went up, Library Street was done away with as a city street
and became simply a pleasant paved passage between the
colleges. But the master's house had to have a street number,
so they gave it what would be the nearest—70 High Street—
with the result that confusion was thereafter confounded. It
was like the rowhouses on numbered streets adjoining Park
Avenue in New York, which claim they are on Park Avenue
when they aren't at all, but are around the corner from it.
The address 70 High was not on High at all, but on a
walkway that went off from it.

During one of the many periods at the beginning of
World War II when I had no help whatever, and was struggling alone to keep our family ship afloat, I was down in the

basement doing the laundry one morning when the front doorbell rang. I dashed up the stairs, drying my sudsy arms and rolling down my sleeves as I went.

A bewildered, middle-aged, not-too-bright-looking woman stood there, and immediately poured out a pitiful tale of her vain efforts to find number 70 High Street. Jonathan Edwards' master's house at that address had advertised for a cook, and she was trying to answer the ad, but all these buildings looked just alike to her, and the big closed gates and stone walls had her completely baffled. Could I help her? Would I?

I didn't blame the poor soul for being confused. Better men than she had walked around in circles there. When I started trying to explain about the number 70 not being on High but on Library, which did not even exist, she became more confused than ever.

"Was this, where we were standing, a Yale house?"

Yes, but not the one she was trying to find. This was 80; she wanted 70, and it wasn't even on High. All my well-meant directions only confused her the more. In the intricacies of telling her how to get to a place that not only wasn't on the street where it said it was, but was somewhere else on a street that wasn't even a street, I mixed both of us up hopelessly.

"Oh dear," she wailed, "I'll never find it!"

"No," I said to myself, "from my directions, you never will," and added impulsively, "Come along with me. We'll go through this house and I'll take you there. It is only a step this way."

She followed gratefully through the office and out into the court, and as she panted along behind me, asked fearfully, "What's the work like in these college places? I hear that it's dreadful hard, that they have lots of company."

"Nonsense, don't you believe it! Working here is quite pleasant," I assured her. "They have all the most modern kitchen equipment, beautiful monel metal things, all very nice."

"You really like your job?" she asked earnestly.

The light broke: she thought I was the maid at number 80.

"I love it," I answered her truthfully, and added, also truthfully, "You couldn't pay me to work anywhere else!"

Why in the world didn't I have sense enough to snag her for my own maidless kitchen? But the Jonathan Edwards master's wife was my friend, and we didn't play dirty tricks on each other. I delivered her safely to number 70 and went sadly back to the laundry in number 80.

Potential cooks are not the only ones who got lost both inside and outside these walls. Most visitors to New Haven wanted to see the famous Harkness Quadrangle, and managed somehow to get in, but not always to get out again.

A delicate decision often needed to be made about people seen wandering around in the court. That man who seemed to be as lonely as a cloud might be an alumnus accompanied by happy memories and ghosts, dreaming dreams of other years as he "walks beside the reverend walls in which of old he wore the gown." If this were so, he wanted no interruption.

On the other hand, he might be a complete stranger in New Haven, or a lonely alumnus who had wandered around for some time without running into anyone he knew, and be quite prepared to go back to Cleveland, or Miami, or Dallas, disillusioned about Yale's continuing need of him. Everyone he knew had either departed or was busy; nobody took any notice of him, the new buildings confused him so that he didn't feel at home anymore. He vowed to himself that never again would he make the mistake of going back to New Haven. His wandering around alone was a real catastrophe for both him and the university, and perhaps a tentative, "Could I help you locate someone?" or, "Have you seen the little chapel under the tower?" would give a whole new tone to his visit. I have stood at the window many a time, wondering whether I dared go out and accost some seemingly distressed and bewildered visitor.

Although the front door opening on the street was supposed always to be locked, occasionally some one of us might forget to put the latch back on, and an innocent but curious passerby, finding the door unlocked, would happen in.

One evening before dinner, Steve and I were in the living room when we heard the front door open, and a man's deep voice say, "Let's go in here. It's all right, Walter; you come too." Whoever these people were, they proceeded to move around in the hall, evidently examining the pictures and furniture; then a group of three persons appeared at the living room door, and were completely taken aback at seeing us there.

"Why, there are people here," the deep voice said in consternation. "I beg your pardon. We didn't know there would be anyone."

"Yes, we are here," my husband said, rising, "but do come in. We are happy to have you here too."

The poor man was covered with confusion. He and his

wife and their chauffeur were on their way to Boston, and never having seen Yale, he decided to swing by and give it a look. They had no idea that any of these great downtown buildings were private homes; he could not apologize enough for bursting in on us.

At our insistence, he and his wife stayed for a pleasant half-hour and a glass of sherry. Then he said that they must go, as they were leaving for Mexico City the next day, and still had a few things to see to.

"That is a coincidence," my husband told him. "The last people in this room, who left only a few minutes before you came, and to whose leaving the door open we are indebted to meeting you, were my sister and her husband who came to say goodbye before starting for a new home in Mexico City. Her husband is to teach at the university."

"We are old-time residents," our unexpected guest said. "We have kept an apartment there for a long time, where we try to spend at least half of every year. I shall be happy to get in touch with your sister and her husband, if you will give me their names."

He was as good as his word, and was extremely helpful to the Johnsons during their first weeks in a strange city and country. A month later, an autographed photograph arrived of him and his wife, Steve's sister and her husband, all smiling broadly, and seated cosily around a table at Ciro's.

There were so many entrances, archways, and gates within the Quadrangle that strangers wandering in frequently were confused. Answering a buzz at the office door one afternoon after the secretary had gone, I found a mother and her two young sons.

"We are lost," she said. "We don't seem to find a door

out that leads to the street. I am sure we could if we kept looking, but our train is due soon, and I am getting a little panicky. Will you help us get to High Street?"

I brought them through the house as the shortest way, telephoned for a taxi, and because the house was simply reeking with the delicious odor of freshly baked cookies, brought out a plateful for the boys while they waited. Several years later, at the freshman reception at the president's house, a tall boy stopped as he came down the line, and said, "Remember me? I'm one of those lost boys you gave cookies to three years ago."

Then there were the visitors who just happened by. On a bitter cold afternoon I answered the bell to find a half-frozen young woman shivering there.

"I am from out of town," she said between chattering teeth. "Can you tell me where the guide is who takes people around? He was supposed to meet us under Harkness Tower at three for a tour. It's three-thirty now, no guide has shown up, and I don't know what to do."

"Come in and thaw," I invited, "and I'll telephone somewhere and find out about it."

"There are some people with me," she said hesitatingly.

"Bring them in, too."

She stepped back to the sidewalk, gestured down the street and called, "Yoo-hoo, girls, come in here!" and at least forty young women streamed into our living room.

It was a club of secretaries from Bridgeport, and this sightseeing jaunt to neighbor Yale was their monthly meeting.

I telephoned the guide service and found that the special boy assigned to them had made a mistake about the date and was not to be found, but in fifteen minutes they had another guide at the door. While they waited, since they had lost so much time from what would be his spiel, I told them the story of the building of the quadrangle and its later conversion into two colleges. Steve happened by to get some papers, and was called in and met them all.

As they left, safely under the wing of the new guide, and I apologized again for the breakdown in service, one of them said, "This has been much better! That is the first real dean I've ever met! We never dreamed we'd get inside of anything, or see any of the inmates." These nice young women sent me an invitation to their club meeting the next month, and even offered to pay my transportation both ways.

All of my contacts with the outside world were not with such pleasant people. Shortly after we had moved in a disgruntled woman at the door demanded to know where a certain gateway was. (This wasn't its name, but we'll call it the Pratt Gateway.)

I hadn't the faintest idea; I had never heard of it. All the dozens of gates and entryways had names, carved over them in the stone, but probably the secretary of the university was the only one who knew them all, and where each was. Certainly I didn't. I asked her to come in while I tried to locate it.

"No, I won't come in," she snapped. "My husband and I will sit out here on the wall and wait while you find it."

She was extremely unpleasant about the whole matter, informing me that this gate was named for one of her ancestors, a great benefactor of Yale, and she had no intention of going home to Indianapolis until she had seen it and taken a snapshot of it. She was going to give a paper to her club about this ancestor, and must have the picture. She and her husband were on an excursion to New York, and had made this extra trip up to New Haven just to see and photograph the gate.

"At the time of the Revolution, he made a fortune on manufacturing arms, and gave a great deal of it to Yale," she added in a tone that said plainly that she wished he hadn't. "So they named a gate for him. We have never understood in my family why this place is named Yale and not Pratt University. Apparently it is a case of benefits forgot, if nobody even knows where the gate is."

It was most unfortunate, of course, that I couldn't lead her immediately to her family gate, and find it crowned with laurel. If she had only given me a little notice beforehand! She and her husband seated themselves outside on the low stone wall, and I scurried frantically to the telephone. The secretary wasn't in, of course, and nobody in the office knew off-hand about the whereabouts of this particular gate. There were gates and archways in all ten of the colleges— dozens of them. They could look it up, of course; could they call me back?

In the meantime, I went out into the Branford court to go the rounds and examine all the gates and arches here on the desperate chance that it was somewhere among them. Luck was with me. Not only was it in Branford, but at the office door I ran into one of the bachelor resident Fellows who lived through that very entrance. Jubilant, I scurried back to tell the munition maker's descendant.

She was sitting there on the wall where I had left her, but not *still* sitting—she was sitting *again*, for, impatient of waiting, she too had gone looking for it.

Her poor husband was almost beside himself. "I *told* her to wait for you, but no, she decided to go and find it herself, and she has twisted her ankle." It was visibly swelling.

But be the ankle twisted, sprained, or broken entirely with splinters of bone sticking out, that woman was determined to get a picture of the gate, and when I told her that I now knew where it was, right here in our own courtyard, she leaned on me and her husband, and in what must have been excruciating pain, went through the house and around to the gate and snapped her picture.

"Where is the life-sized statue of Yale?" her husband then asked me. "While we're here, I'd like to see that."

This was certainly my day for knowing none of the answers, but this time the interrogator hadn't known the question, and I could scarcely be blamed for not knowing where this one was, since it didn't exist.

"I'm afraid—" I began, but he cut me short.

"You live here," he said in scornful amazement, "and don't even know where the famous statue of Nathan Yale is!"

Other people have perhaps confused Nathan Hale and Elihu Yale, but I had never happened to run into one before.

On a few occasions, visitors might even be dangerous. During the course of a year, my husband often had a number of unpleasant interviews with difficult students, but most of them took place in his office, and he didn't even tell me of them. But one night, after I had gone upstairs to bed, a loud, angry voice at the front door announced himself as a boy who I knew had been causing a good bit of trouble to the administration. He was definitely mentally unbalanced, and the psychiatry department had urged him to withdraw from the university, but he was determined to do no such thing.

Now here he was in our front hall at eleven o'clock at night, shouting that he had something to say, and that my husband had better listen to him say it.

My husband was quite calm, as he took him into the living room, and they began to talk. I, on the other hand, as terrified as I have ever been in my life, crept fearfully down the stairs to sit in the dark dining room adjacent to where they were, a heavy candlestick grasped for a weapon in a trembling hand. I don't know quite what I expected to do with it—probably I would try to whack him over the head if he attacked my husband—but I felt safer being "armed."

Fortunately I didn't have to use it. For a long time a low steady murmur of talk went on in the living room. Gradually the angry voice had calmed down, and eventually there was even a laugh or two. After what seemed to me an interminable length of time, they came out to the door, and with a friendly handshake the boy said goodnight and left.

After he had gone quietly away, I felt very silly holding my "weapon," but in view of the meeting a few years later that just such another student sought with Dr. Thorne, and its fatal termination, my candlestick wasn't really so foolish.

15

While we lived in the suburbs we kept our Christmas tree outdoors in the cold until Christmas Eve, at which time it was brought in and the evening given to trimming it. But students went home about December 18, and in order to give a more festive air to those last days here for them, we committed the sacrilege of trimming and lighting our tree early. As they went by in the court to dinner, it was nice for them to see the lit tree shining out through the windows those last few evenings. It took the edge off for us, of course, to have it up so long, but we were reconciled to having the edge taken off things occasionally for their sakes.

So up it went, and everybody in the family was ready to help in the decoration. There were willing loopers of strings of lights, eager hangers of the same old ornaments, a lively argument about angel or star for the very top place; somebody was ready with the new box of candycanes and freshly baked gingerbread men; somebody else was draping sleet or hanging icicles. A few fragile colored balls, grasped too firmly, were sure to be crushed, with cries of "Oops! sorry, there goes another one!" Even the cat slithered around through the lower branches and gave a tentative pat at a few balls. It was a gay, noisy scene.

But this change in the trimming date meant that in spite of having its foot in a bucket of water (flavored with the recommended maple syrup and aspirin), because the tree went up early the needles began to fall early too, and it could not wait until the traditional date of twelfth night to come down.

And when coming-down date arrived, with Christmas furor over, all those willing trimmers were nowhere to be found. No one, no one at all, helped with the deflowering. All alone, in the pitiless, glamorless glare of ten o'clock in the morning, I brought out the big boxes these gaudy things lived in all year and went at my solitary annual job of entangling myself in light cords, pricking fingers on a few sharp-edged broken balls, packing all the little ornaments in their little nests for another year. Candycanes and gingerbread men had completely vanished. Needles were falling fast around me at even the feather touch of a finger to a branch; I hated to think of the train of them I was going to leave when I dragged the denuded tree through the house and down the basement stairs, where the indignity of being chopped up and burned in the building incinerator was awaiting it.

I was bemoaning all this on one such after-Christmas morning when the weekly cleaning man, Dick, came roaring through the hall with the vacuum (which he always accompanied with a low rendition of "Lead on, O King Eternal"), saw my predicament, and generously offered his help.

"Just leave it to me. You get all the trimming off, and I'll take care of the tree."

I gladly accepted. I carried off to the storeroom the big

boxes of trimming and pushed them back on a top shelf until another Christmas should roll around, and never gave the tree another thought. That evening, with every needle carefully swept away, the living room seemed very bare with no reminder of recent celebration; Christmas was over; it was a new year.

It was almost two weeks later that while in the living room one afternoon, I happened to glance out of the window at the regular daily tour of sightseers walking slowly through the court, following the Yale guide. They were all looking my way, evidently attracted by something near the house. I went over to the window to see what it could be.

To my horror, I looked right down into the upturned face, you might say, of the wreck of a spruce tree, lying close against the building at a rakish angle, half upside down, a few bedraggled ribbons of forgotten silver foil sleet waving feebly in the wind—unmistakably our late Christmas tree, pitched out of the window. It had been there almost two weeks, for hundreds of returning students to see three times a day as they passed to the dining hall, and for heaven knows how many sightseers to gaze at in disgust as they toured the place.

It was easy to see how it had happened, but of course, that was no excuse. Rather than leave a path of needles through the house, Dick had wisely decided to put the tree through the window, and bring it to the incinerator through an outside basement door. He had thrown it out, and then tidied the living room to the soothing hum of the vacuum cleaner and his usual hymn accompaniment. With the tree out of sight, it was completely out of mind as well. He vacuumed the rest of the house and went home, and like me he never gave the tree another thought.

No student ever said a word about that tree either to my husband or to me. They probably thought that that was what *we* thought you did with an old Christmas tree.

WHEN THE Christmas holidays actually came, and there was a general exodus, my first feeling was joy for a little privacy at last. But soon the emptiness and silence of the courts, and the darkness at night of a hundred windows usually lighted, began to bother me. It was too silent, too dark! And there is no place on earth more desolate than an empty college dormitory. I missed these boys whose constant presence and requests usually ran me ragged!

But they hadn't all gone home. There were always a few whose parents lived abroad or at any rate too far away for them to afford the trip for such a short time, or to whom it would have been an inconvenience to have them just then. These left-behinders were scattered through the dormitories—perhaps an entire hall would have only one lone vacation tenant. Some of them found jobs in the post office, or on the wall-washing gang that went through the colleges during vacation and did the spring cleaning of woodwork and windows. They had a long work day, and came back tired at night to a lonesome room. The dining halls were closed; the boys kept themselves alive on peanut butter and canned baked beans, or picked up hamburgers and pizzas at some restaurant or greasy-spoon in the town. I was sure they were not getting the right kind of food, or enough. Old Mother Hen began to worry about how grim it must be for them.

Perhaps I was being a sentimental softie; my husband said I was. His withers were not at all wrung. He definitely needed this rest from students for a while, and welcomed it. He liked the restful darkness in all those windows; what I called loneliness, he considered peace on earth.

We always collected those we could find for Christmas Day dinner, but the head of the house positively refused to spend all of his precious vacation days boy-sitting. He considered that the usual tea on holiday Sunday afternoons, and the one big festive meal on the day itself, were enough for us to do for them.

But I worried about the other meals, and days, and nights, and wondered if I couldn't do something to make Christmas a little merrier, or at least less grim, for the solitary lights that shone out here and there at night. So whenever someone in the town, or among the faculty, called me with an invitation for a dinner, or a Christmas party for "any boys who are around," I accepted enthusiastically, and knocked myself out trying to get hold of them. This was not too easy, for if they were not at work, they were apt to be at a movie or else so sound asleep in their rooms that the telephone ring meant nothing, and many didn't even have phones by which they could be reached. Invariably I got into hot water whenever I relayed such bids, and sometimes I got the boys into hot water too, but it seemed that I never learned. One thing, however, I did learn—that a request from a hostess with a daughter, for "any boys who are around," really meant "any tall, handsome, rich team captains who dance divinely." When the boys I sent her instead were a shy lad from the Tennessee backcountry, with pimples and two big left feet, and a little Chinese boy who hadn't mastered English yet, the warmth of hospitality offered cooled perceptibly.

Once a vacation invitation came from a big pleasant

home far out in the country where there were no entangling daughters. It would get these students out of too-quiet dormitory rooms, give them a taste of family life, and more than a taste, I trusted, of a big noon family dinner. I pulled out my student telephone directory and went to work dialing. At the end of thirty calls to the rooms of boys with home addresses at least five hundred miles away, I had found three who answered, one with a roommate also here, and I passed along the invitation. They were delighted to accept. They were picked up by their host at our front door. I patted myself on the back; I had done a really good deed.

The boys came in the next day to report on how it all went. First, accustomed to the well-heated university buildings they almost froze to death, the whole house being kept at a steady sixty-three degrees for the health of a tangle of beagles who had the run of the place. Second, since there was no bus line near, they were a band of captives, unable to leave when they wanted to, and completely dependent for their getaway on their host, who got in the only car and drove off somewhere after dinner to see a man about a dog, and on his return went upstairs and was taking a nap before anyone knew he was back and available as a chauffeur. Third, and not least, besides the dogs, the house was also overrun with tiny terrors of grandchildren, whose parents must have been farming them out with indulgent grandparents until such time as they should be old enough to meet the age requirement for the state reformatory.

Two days later their hostess telephoned me "to tell me her side," which had an ominous sound. One boy, looking down his nose at practically every dish offered, announced that he was allergic to anything containing butter or cooked with salt. Another had an aversion to dogs, having been badly bitten in childhood, he said. (And the house *was* home to about eight beagles.)

The afternoon was marred considerably by the lack of unanimity on the hour at which the boys felt their visit should terminate, a rather important matter, since they were a long way out in the country, with no bus line near. They had neglected to get together on this before they left the college, and now one of them said he simply had to get back early to do some work on a paper that was already overdue. Another had nothing at all on hand, and was more than willing to stay for cold turkey sandwiches for supper, and even showed a rather frightening inclination to be adopted for the entire vacation. All named different hours at which, and not before nor after, it was vitally necessary they should be returned to the college.

I resolved after that to stick to bus lines. What I should have resolved was always to let boys handle their own social engagements. But no, with the kindest intentions in the world, I must meddle again.

A warm-hearted woman, anxious to dispense hospitality to lonely college students far from home and loved ones, telephoned that she was giving a supper party for her daughter's crowd, and would love to have any of our students who were still around to join them. She was taking the whole group to the dance at the Lawn Club afterwards.

I knew this woman only slightly, but the two facts that I knew about her were that she had a pretty daughter at Wellesley, and a lovely home *in town, right on a bus line.* (I never made the same mistake twice; always new mistakes.) This sounded foolproof to me.

I got in touch with one of our juniors that I knew quite well, who had told me he was flat broke during the holidays, and to whom a free good supper and evening of dancing would appeal. He wasn't rich, or the football captain, but he was a real charmer, and I didn't see how this time I could possibly go wrong. He said he knew two other boys who would be delighted to go too. I asked him to be sure to come in afterwards and tell me about it. He did.

"You got out of this very well," he began. "*You* made only one enemy for life—me. But I've got two, in those two guys I took along."

To begin with, the party wasn't for the Wellesley daughter at all, who it seems had married that year and moved away, but for a high school sophomore daughter that I didn't even know existed, and her very juvenile crowd.

"A hoary thirteen years old, if they were a day," snorted my college junior.

The good free supper party I had congratulated myself on steering three hungry boys to was hot dogs, potato chips, lots of tomato ketchup, and Coca-Colas. Then they piled in cars and went to the club. When they got there, the majority of the party said, "Hello, Brad," to the ticket-taker at the door, who was evidently an old friend, and walked blithely in, but when my three boys said, "Hello, Brad," they were firmly halted and told it was three dollars each. Unfortunately, by going off in a corner, and pooling their cash, they were able to raise that much between them.

"Here we made our big mistake," Tom said. "We should have come home."

But instead they went in, expecting their troubles to be over and to find some of their own age group inside.

"The whole thing must have been a school party," the story went on. "The ballroom was filled with the dearest youngsters you ever laid your eyes on. But were they the little wise guys! The hostess's daughter, who danced so close she raised my temperature, kept on yapping about perishing for a drink, and that there were cocktails in the lobby. Finally, I told her that if she was so thirsty, to go down to the ladies' room and get a drink out of the water cooler. I'm not morally degenerate enough to have bought that infant any likker, even if I had had the price of it, which I didn't."

I succeeded eventually in making him take the price of the dance tickets, and entered nine dollars in the family budget book under the heading "Experience."

"From now on," said I to myself, "hostesses can run their parties with ten more girls than boys, for all of me, and boys can languish in loneliness in their rooms over the holidays. Never again will I get myself or anybody else in such trouble!"

So a couple of days before Christmas, when the wife of a friend on the faculty telephoned to know if I could furnish a student escort to a dance for a Smith sophomore who was staying with them, I said immediately, "Nay, nay, Lady!" I related a bit of my former experiences, and said that I had sworn off getting involved in these things; I was definitely no date bureau.

She was properly horrified at my tales, agreed heartily with my resolution, but went on to assure me that in this instance nothing could possibly happen to embarrass either the boy or me. She realized that boys should not be asked to spend money on dates not of their own making, and since this was a favor to her the expense was, of course, all to be hers. This was a dance, she said, given each year by the Faculty Club for Yale sons and daughters home for the holidays, and was quite informal. No, not as informal as blue jeans; she had meant not black tie. She had already bought the tickets. Some of them were to have supper beforehand at the Faculty Club, and that was already ordered and paid for by one of the parents. No money would be needed all evening; every possible contingency had been taken care of; *nothing could go wrong.* All the boy had to do was to come. The girl was even quite pretty and attractive, and the only reason that she was having to be provided with an escort was that she had never visited here before, and knew no one, and the hostess knew no students staying over the holidays.

There popped into my mind a boy from California who was here for the whole vacation, who had a vacation job cleaning the colleges on what they called "the black gang." He was having a pretty slim holiday, with long days of menial work and no fun. Against my better judgment, I finally said I would try to get in touch with him.

He proved to be "on location," or in other words, out at work in one of the buildings, but just which one the work supervisor did not seem to know. It was bitter cold, and raining, but I went from building to building, and at each walked through the dining hall, library, common room, halls, calling for my prey. In the fourth building, on top of a stepladder, I found him at last, and told him the story.

I gave him my friend's promise that this was a completely informal, no-expense tour. He allowed from the top of the stepladder, with a streaming scrub-brush in his hand, that it sounded like fun. Wall-washing was getting a little grim, and he needed to go to a party where there were girls.

I trotted home again in a perfect glow of self-righteousness over the festive evening he was going to have, thanks to me.

The night of the party, a miserable boy came in to see me about half an hour before he was supposed to be at the other end of town at my friend's house to pick up the girl.

"I probably shouldn't come to you," he said, "but I don't know what to do. What I'd like to do is chuck the whole thing, but I feel responsible to you about this, for I promised you. Here's the score: I called up this chick to find out what bus to take out there, and she was bowled over to learn that I didn't have a car. She said that she thought that *everybody* had a car! She must have decided that if I didn't have one, I was right out of the backwoods, for she said very coolly, 'I don't suppose I have to ask you if you are wearing a tuxedo?' I said that I had understood that this was informal. She said that 'informal' meant only that the girls didn't wear strapless dresses. Besides, this gang that we are to have supper with turns out to be 'the committee,' and is apparently something rather special, and 'the committee' all wear tuxedos, even if some of the common footsoldiers at the dance won't have them on.

"Now, what do I do next? I haven't a car; I don't own a tux. There isn't anybody around here to borrow from, and at seven o'clock on Christmas Eve, I can't rent one. I don't mind so much letting this Smithie down, but I don't want to go back on you."

What I wanted to tell him to do was to go to the movies

and forget the whole thing, but I too felt I couldn't go back on a friend. ("Will you never, never learn to keep out of other people's business?" I said to myself.)

My victim said that his roommate, who was on a skiing jaunt for the holidays, had left a tuxedo in his closet, and that if he only knew how to get in touch with him, which he didn't, he was sure he could borrow it. Burglary seemed of very small account in this emergency. Hoping that heaven would forgive me, and that no one else, especially my husband, would ever find out, I gave Phil my grand master key which would open his roommate's closet door, and sent him back on his nefarious errand.

I telephoned my friend to explain that he would be a little late—no car, and a little trouble about the tuxedo. She was speechless with surprise about the car. How stupid of her! For she too had taken it for granted that he would have a car. Not to worry. She would drive them herself to the club, or if he had a license, he could take her car. The girl was absolutely mistaken about all the boys wearing tuxedos. She had chaperoned this dance in other years, and while there were some tuxedos there, the large majority did not wear them. Perhaps "the committee" usually did, but on this occasion she knew positively that one of them at least would not, for he and his father shared a suit, and the father, with priority, was wearing it at a dinner in New York that night. She was sorry that the boy had not talked to *her* on the phone instead of the girl. There was *nothing* to be concerned about.

In the meantime, Phil had been doing a neat job of breaking and entering, and returned to me resplendent in his roommate's dinner clothes, which fitted him well enough, if not perfectly.

There was no fairytale ending, such as, "And would you believe it? Three years later they were married the day after his graduation, and her father made him vice-president of one of his companies." But after the rocky beginning, the rest of the evening passed off quite happily and Phil had a good time. The roommate didn't come back unexpectedly, and as he frequently drove the family car at home, Phil did have a driver's license. At the end of the evening, he drove the Smithie and her hostess's car safely home, and since the buses had stopped running by then, had a long walk himself back to the college.

The next morning he was at his job, cleaning walls, and best of all, he didn't hate me forever. As a matter of fact, sharing the secret of our burglary was a bond that made us good friends. Once more, I vowed never, never would I meddle again. And I kept that vow ever afterward.

Sending boys out into the wide world to galas in unknown homes, however, was completely different from leaving them to stay quietly in our own house. We were planning to spend the week after Christmas in Virginia with relatives, and surely the simple thing to do was to have a couple of the left-behind students we knew well stay in the house while we were away, not for any jollification, but simply to take care of our animals and fend off burglars. They could keep food in our icebox and use the kitchen to cook for themselves, and so have real meals at much less cost than eating out would be. I had in mind two Western boys we both knew well—steady, dependable boys, who would really appreciate spending that week in more cheerful quarters than the deserted dormitory.

My husband, however, was far from convinced that it was a good idea. He thought it would be better to have them come in every day to feed the animals and take Nancy for a walk, but not to move over to live in the house, with icebox and pantry at their disposal. He was more hard-hearted than I was over letting boys rough it on occasion. But Christmas, I pointed out, was a season of "good will to men" and I was sure this would be a proper way to celebrate it. I kept urging the plan on him, arguing that the animals would be lonely too, and having someone in the house, and lights on at night would be a protection against intruders. The boys I suggested were short of cash, and this would be a godsend to them.

Everything I said was true, and finally he gave in. The invitation was extended, and joyfully accepted.

We had expected to get back late on the afternoon of New Year's Day, but with good weather, made better time than we had hoped for, and so instead arrived about eleven o'clock that morning, and walked in, quite unexpected, on two very, very busy boys, still cleaning up from a little party held the night before to usher in the new year. They had been hard at cleaning up ever since the last guest left about 4:00 A.M.

It would be difficult to say who were the more surprised as we unexpectedly confronted each other—the students, or the master's family.

What a party that must have been! Long afterward I was still running into people who were there, who would say to me rather cautiously, "Oh, by the way, that Christmas that you were gone and let students stay in your house, did you ever hear about the New Year's Eve party that they gave?" And then a little more would leak out that we hadn't known before. The girls who came, it seems, were called on the phone and told that there was a party at the Branford master's house; until they got there they thought *we* were giving it! All the lights were on, some of the windows open, and music of one sort or another blaring forth, and as the night wore on, any students, or friends of students, or friends of friends of students, or just friendly people who happened to be passing, were welcomed in to join the gaiety. Boys sat at the telephone in the hall, trying to think of the names of other people to ask to come over.

I never really learned everything that went on, and perhaps it was just as well, but I know that there were bare footprints on the piano top, and pieces of broken glasses (not eyeglasses) all over the house, upstairs and down, and right in the middle of the front hall rug, where it stared you in the eye the minute you came in the door, was a great yellow ring, like a sunburst. It was so awful, and so conspicuous, that we had to replace the rug, which was wall to wall, and ran all the way up the front stairs.

This was one of the few things that the two boys felt called upon to explain to us. "It was just an unfortunate accident," they said in chorus, "and no one's fault, really."

It seems that one of the jovial guests, rummaging through the food left in the icebox, came on the remains of a carton of eggs, and immediately had the bright idea of putting one in the overcoat pocket of each male guest as he left. It would be slipped in unbeknownst, in the midst of the confusion of departure, and later it would really be hilarious when a hand was rammed unsuspectingly down into the pocket that contained the egg. I don't know how many eggs rode intact out of our front door, but in one instance, the boy felt someone fumbling at his pocket, and jerked around. The egg fell in the middle of the hall floor. The new rug cost $412.

In extenuation, I must say that other students had come in and simply taken over from the two we had left there, and the party as it turned out was not at all the simple and even nonalcoholic one they had planned. Neither of them had ever been host to a party before, and they were too inexperienced and unsophisticated to know that of all parties, one on New Year's Eve was the kind most likely to get out of control. They were both horrified at what had happened, expected expulsion at the very least, and were overcome with gratitude at the understanding way my husband handled the whole incident. I was willing to bet that it would be many a long year before either of these two boys again gave a New Year's Eve party. Certainly they would never have the chance to give one again in our house.

I learned something, too. There is such a thing as taking "good will to men" too far. And I never did like the new rug as much as the old.

16

Before 1942, most American homes at our financial level had felt that domestic help of one—or even two—people was a necessity. Then along came World War II and both men and women were lured away from domestic work and into factories by salaries no home could match, and by the added satisfaction that they were being patriotic. Domestic help—or the lack of it—became the topic of conversation of the housewives of the land. In a *Mirror of Washington* article, I ran across this:

What do they talk about at these luncheons at which the guest of honor is the wife of the president of the United States? Well, even as you and I, the "servant problem" nearly always seems to creep into the chitchat. At a recent luncheon in honor of the president's wife, some of the best stories concerned the cook.

Anyone who had ever kept house in those days could write a book about her cooks, just as I am perfectly sure that anyone who has ever been a cook could write an equally— perhaps more—interesting one about the houses where she has worked.

Before we moved into a master's house, we had been

living too far in the suburbs for casual dropping-in, and had no responsibility whatever for university entertaining. When we moved on campus, all that changed. Casual dropping-in was the rule, not the exception; we had a real load of responsibility for university entertaining, and life often seemed one party after another. The help situation was bleakness itself, for the cook we had had in the country had just remarried and retired from the job world to keep house for her new husband, and the children's nurse (a neighbor girl who had been with us five years), went into a hairdressing school. The previous master's staff had simply disappeared. The butler went into the Winchester factory to make guns, where besides guns he made so much money that his elderly wife, who had been the 80 High Street cook, retired to a rocking chair on their front porch.

Anyone who could pat her foot could get a factory job for twice what housework paid; everyone in New Haven who had a maid was holding on to her like grim death, and the only maids floating around, jobless, were definitely what an old woman I once knew called "the rift and the raft." Most people simply rolled up their sleeves and took care of their own homes; the slogan "do it yourself" became popular.

But I simply had to have some help. The responsibility of entertaining for Yale sat heavily on me; my children were very young, two of them only toddlers; I didn't myself know very much about cooking, and didn't like what little I knew. Just the realization that at the end of the day, the long, tiring, busy day, would come inevitably *dinner*, was enough to discourage me from the time I woke up onward. If dinner only had come immediately after breakfast, say at nine-thirty or even ten, when I still had some enthusiasm about life, I might have been able to manage it, but at the day's end, what a ghastly time to be called upon to cope.

During those first years in New Haven, a long procession of so-called "help" wound through the Branford master's house. Anyone who lasted a month was regarded as an old family retainer; sometimes I couldn't put up with them; sometimes they walked out on me.

They all had two things in common: not a one of them was ever the size of any other one—which meant a constant purchasing of new uniforms—and not a one of them could ever get a message straight. Telephone calls went something like this:

"Somebody called while you were out. She said for you to call her as soon as you came in."

"I'll do it right now. Who was it?"

A pause. "Well, that's a funny thing. I was sure I'd remember her name."

"But you wrote it down?"

"No, I was so sure I'd remember it that there wasn't any reason to write it down. Do you know anybody named Lanscrat or Whoosuff or something like that?"

"Of course I don't. But she gave you her telephone number?"

"Oh, yes, she told me the number—twice."

"Don't tell you didn't write *that* down?"

"I didn't have to write it down, because it was easy to remember." A beaming smile; everything was going to be all right!

"Well, let's have it."

"Seven-eight-five . . . no, it was six-eight-five . . . well, isn't that funny? I declare, I was sure I'd remember that number! It was something like four-eight-five-three-five-zero-nine; I know there was a five in it somewhere!"

"Did she leave any message?" I would ask desperately. "Perhaps I can figure out from that who it was."

"Yes. She said to tell you that it was real important, and to call her right back as soon as you came in."

Lucille was an excellent cook, and such an honest-looking creature that I took her sorrows to myself and tried to alleviate them. She and her husband were living in a miserable, crowded rooming house, where eighteen people used one bathroom. She had heard of apartment houses where her husband could be janitor in return for the rent of a basement apartment, and it was her dream to find one, but neither of them knew how to go about doing it. My home was so pleasant, and hers must have been unspeakable; I had a bathroom to myself, and every time I went into it my conscience smote me as I thought of poor Lucille waiting in a long line in the hall to use hers, so in pity I went to a rental agency for her and asked if they had such positions as the one I described.

"Sometimes we do," the receptionist replied, without losing the place in the magazine she was reading. "Sit down over there and fill out this form. How old is your husband? Has he ever done janitorial work before?"

I brightened my husband's dinner with that one.

The apartment house job didn't turn up, but finally by pulling strings and practically perjuring myself I got Lucille and her husband into one of the little apartments in the new housing development in Westville. She wept with delight, and was *so* grateful, and said they would never forget what I had done for them, and gave me notice, saying it was too far to come to work anymore. (It was fifteen minutes on the bus line.)

True to form, the next incumbent didn't fit into Lucille's uniforms, nor in any of the large stack which I had by now amassed from predecessors, so I had to make a shopping trip for more. "I hope this will be the right size," I said, half to myself, holding one up, and trying to visualize Carline in it. She had told me she thought she wore a twelve, but I knew she could no more wear a twelve than Kate Smith could. The salesgirl was very kind.

"Why don't you go in the dressing room and try it on, dear?" she suggested helpfully.

Then came Clara. She was a smart young girl about twenty, jolly and good-humored, and a bang-up cook, slapping things together in jig time by rule of thumb, without benefit of cookbook or measures of any kind. Oh, her fresh peach pies! Her rice puddings, that even the children, who proverbially loathe rice puddings, begged for. Her thin little biscuits that melted in your mouth!

She had a brother in the army, stationed in Italy.

"What does Charlie write you about Italy?" I asked her one day. "Does he think it is interesting to be assigned there?"

"He doesn't think much of it," she answered. "He says Italy isn't anything but a lot of old torn-down buildings, and a mountain that's been spewing up."

I would have kept Clara forever if she would have stayed, for not only was she a natural-born cook, but she had the gift of silence. I didn't have to waste my time chatting with her, or listening to her, as is so often the case where there is only one servant and she gets lonely. Clara had plenty of excitement in her life without being dependent on any of my tame conversation. But she went the way of all flesh at that time—into the Winchester factory, and it finished the payments on the fur coat that we started for her.

For a time while Clara was there I had also an aged woman who came in to do the ironing—Maggie, who wore a startling red wig. She was rather an old dear, but about a one-mouse-power worker; you had to sight her against something to be sure she was moving. She was in that always desirable state for household help, a "widow-woman with no followers." In contrast to Clara's silence, she was the out-talkingest woman I ever met. All day long she kept it up— the likes and dislikes of her departed husbands in the matter of food, her nephew in Jersey City who was a dentist, her sister who played the piano at church, her father who had been a waiter at the Parker House in Boston, her son who had died at the age of twenty.

To keep this talker happy, somebody had to be listening to her all the time. After Clara left I had the bright thought of putting the dog to work as chief listener, and Nancy did a magnificent job. She wagged and woofed at the right places, and occasionally was so overcome by the narrative that the only way she could express her feelings was to roll over and put all four paws in the air.

One of the prizes that I drew as a maid about this time was Annie, an Irish girl whose greatest characteristic, in contrast to poor one-mouse-power Maggie, was speed. Quickness I regarded as a great virtue, and for its sake I would put up with many other things. Annie moved so fast that she was inclined forward all the time. She carried a pail of soapy water guaranteed to take the finish off any floor, and a perfect jack-straw tangle of mops and broom handles and carpet sweepers wherever she went, frequently falling over them herself and often leaving them in places where they were most likely to trip up the rest of us. She was in residence one week only. I shouldn't say "in residence," for she lived at home, and came to work when she got good and ready.

On Monday she came, on Tuesday she didn't, on Wednesday she reported at noon, on Thursday—supposedly her day off—she was violently ringing the doorbell and beating on the panels of the back door with her fists at 6:00 A.M. because "she wanted to get started early," as she had also planned to leave early.

I remonstrated. "Annie, let's get this straight. Just exactly what do you understand your hours to be?"

She turned on me with this withering comment: "I'm a free Amurican citizen, and I work when I please."

Her stay was short, and she left by request, but for at least a year, prospective employers would call me up and say that Annie had given me as a reference.

For a while we hired a chubby little thing who said she wanted me to get it straight right at the start that she did not belong to "the servant class," was a college student, and was only taking the job temporarily in order to make the dues for her sorority. She wore a large wooden lapel pin in the shape of a monkey, with "Don't monkey with me!" on it in large letters. She spent most of her time doing her nails in the servants' dining room and translating Spanish.

And there was dear Hilda, a hefty Finn, who could not read, write, speak, or understand English. I didn't know any more Finnish than she did English, but I bought a little Finnish-English dictionary and we struggled along together with it. Not being able to tell whether a jar contained salt, pepper, mustard, mace, or rat poison if there was no guiding picture, she went wholly by instinct, and this made eating a real adventure for the few days that she lit up our hearth. For light it up she certainly did, being gleamingly clean about her person, and smiling so brightly with a full set of gold teeth that the house was perceptibly darker when she left.

She leaped to answer the telephone and doorbell, and sent everyone away completely mystified. Unfortunately English was not the only thing she did not know—cooking was another. For her first meal, which was Saturday lunch, the children were to have, among other things, blueberry muffins and Jell-o. I got out the utensils for her.

She made the Jell-o in the cast iron muffin pan, and baked the cannonballs in the individual aluminum molds, and I shall never forget as long as I live coming into the kitchen just in time to see her dancing around the stove, taking those little hot molds out of the oven.

I never expect cooks to be able to bake a cake, and I had bought a ten-inch cake from the faculty club to last the family through the week—the week that Annie, the free Amurican citizen, was also with us as upstairs girl and helper. Hilda cut that huge layer cake in four parts, and served Steve and me each a quarter with our ice cream. We regarded each other over the mountains of cake, then he solemnly cut a slice off his piece for me, and another for himself. Seized with a terrible presentiment, I rang for Hilda. I was too late. She and Annie had each eaten their entire quarters.

Hilda was so sweet and so spotlessly clean that I couldn't bear to tell her that she couldn't stay. But finally I told her that she didn't cook quite the way we were accustomed to, and she agreed that "in Finland, it was different." So I bowed her out, both of us bobbing and smiling to each other to the last, and both insisting over and over, so as not to hurt the other's feelings, that things were certainly different in Finland.

Lucetta was a dream to look upon, a sleek and svelte wraith, with an up-swept hairdo, French heels, and the crispest of organdie aprons (which she furnished herself), the gentlest, most charming voice and manner. But she not only wouldn't do laundry—nobody ever would!—she refused to cook, or even try to. But she had been trained to serve at table, and she answered the door beautifully, and because I was rather desperate most of the time by then and turning around like a teetotum trying to get everything done that had to be done in a family and large house, upon which guests were constantly descending, I kept her just to answer the door, to iron the little girls' dresses, and to serve dinner. I cooked the meals and then, hot and out of temper, I was served by Lucetta, cool and fresh and lovely. I did the laundry in the basement, while Lucetta sat in a rocking chair by the kitchen windows watching the boys come out of Yale station across the street, reading comic books, and waiting for the bell to ring.

When it did—and it always did—she would come to the top of the basement stairs and inform me in her flutelike voice that I had a caller. And I would come dashing up the back stairs to my room, skin into another dress, give my hair a lick, and float serenely down the front stairs to spend an hour chatting as if I didn't have a care in the world.

Many others darkened our doors temporarily. There was

one who was so satisfactory in every way, and she liked us and the place so well, that we hoped to spend the rest of our lives together. But alas, a jealous husband, from whom, she confessed to me, she had fled and thought to leave behind forever, found out her address through relatives, and appeared in High Street one day, and invited her to come out.

She cowered in the house for several days, afraid to venture out back to her apartment, while he patrolled the street, shouting to her every now and then, evading the police by hiding in an unlocked parked car or slipping away completely when they came. He had so terrified the poor woman that she said she would always be afraid in New Haven, and that she was going to New York to live. "It's so big, he'll never find me there."

There were many others, including one woman who stayed with us almost ten years, but the usual term of office was short and rarely sweet. Telling about them is more amusing than living with them often was.

Eventually I learned that if you didn't have anybody in the kitchen, you survived. Food that I cooked could be eaten, if not with positive pleasure then at least with safety. I learned to run the house and the children, after a fashion, single-handed, when I had to, and to prefer my own inefficiency to a servant's. I found in my diary of that period this entry: "I haven't had a cook for three weeks; the house is a pool of peace."

17

*L*ife in a master's house was always interesting, never dull, and although exhausting at times, the rewards were many.

For me, the greatest one was getting to know intimately so many splendid boys.

Perhaps the next in importance was the annual cycle in which our lives moved, different from that of the private citizen, which usually jogs along more or less the same, year after year. Each twelve months we were brought up short, as everything came to an abrupt halt, and a third of our "family" left us. A definite "finished" was put to a chapter in our lives, and then we had the privilege, not given to everyone in this naughty world, of taking a deep breath and making a new beginning.

The new year began for us not in January but in the fall. We came back to Yale from our summer home every September before the students got there, in order to be ready for them. I think this was the only time that I begrudged them a bit of my life; it was hard to give up those crisp autumn days in Vermont.

But once back, we were swept along in the enthusiasm of the flood of students who came pouring across the street from freshman Old Campus dormitories to their new address. Last year's sophomores moved up a peg to make room; former juniors now took top ranking as seniors—and occasionally felt a twinge of sentiment as they realized that they were going through the events on the college calendar for the last time.

College days are happy ones, and students proverbially a carefree lot, yet we older people in the masters' houses knew that before this year we were beginning—before any one of our years there—was over, there would be sadness for a few out of our three hundred boys, and so for us. These things bound us together. At least one of them would have lost a family member, or perhaps his own life. A single year brought us these three tragedies:

The parents of a boy who died during the summer before his senior year came to hold a little "graveside service" with the college chaplain, and scatter their son's ashes in the court. The boy had told them that he had passed the happiest years of his life here, and he wanted to be at Yale forever.

Another student, distraught when he received word that his fiancée was one of those who perished in the Cocoanut Grove Club fire, paced the floor in our living room until time for my husband to drive him to the Boston train.

The trunk of an entering sophomore arrived and sat in the hall outside his room for a week. The boy never showed up. Finally there arrived a letter from his father; alone in the house only a few hours before he was to leave for New Haven, he and the house were blown up by escaping gas in the basement.

THE FIRST thing I did on coming back for the new school year was to take last year's freshman yearbook, and try to put together in my mind the faces and names of the hundred or so new boys who would be coming to live in my husband's college, so that when we passed in the courts, I could greet they by name—to their amazement, as they would have no idea who *I* was! I didn't succeed completely, of course, for they were too big a number to master at one gulp, but at least it was a start, to be completed as the opportunities of encountering them individually came up.

When the new year's work began with a renascence of energy and interest, there seemed to stretch ahead of us long months in which to carry out plans, and to improve on last year. And then, suddenly, before we knew it, the year had slipped by and it was June, and our seniors were leaving to scatter across the world. This was the heartache of living in a college, for with each year's end came the time to say good-bye to the boys we'd had time and opportunity to know best. We were so well-known by so many Yalies that we could never have committed a crime and expected to hide unknown anywhere on earth. Some old Yale boy would be sure to rise from out the tangled jungle or from the ice floe, and greet us with, "Why, Dean and Mrs. B., think of seeing you here!"

But they drifted back more than occasionally—football games brought many—and they kept in touch with letters, and sent wedding announcements, and every December a basketful of Christmas cards with pictures of their children. Many of the very young in these were wearing a white terrycloth bib with a big blue Y in the center—the acknowledgment I sent for every birth announcement.

One major difference between living in a college and in a private home was that all of us there had only a definitely allotted length of time to stay. There was constant moving on, both by students and masters. Three years was any one boy's total term of residence, and the master's appointment was only for five. He might be reappointed, and again reappointed, or he might not be, but three years and five years were the time spans hanging over the heads of all who lived there and this knowledge was bound to color our attitude. So short a stint! The Yale Alma Mater rightly called these "The shortest, gladdest years of life," and so much had to be crowded into them!

As far as the master was concerned, even if there should be reappointments, there would come inevitably a deadline of retirement age at which he would be no longer eligible for the mastership. When this was reached, he must uproot his family, by that time firmly attached to the place, and find them a new home.

This time-sword of Damocles does not hang over the head of people settled in homes of their own. There one may live all of his life in the place where he was born, watch a slim sapling he himself planted grow to a giant tree under which his grandchildren play. There is stability, and a pervading peace. If he dies before his wife, she has a safe haven, perhaps forever, but certainly a place in which to stay until she has time to rearrange her life.

If a college master died in office, the first question asked his widow by her landlord, Yale, (in the kindest of tones, but very firmly) was, "How soon can you get out?" The wheels of the college must continue to turn; the new master has already been decided upon, and his possessions were in a van at the doorstep, waiting to be brought inside.

We lived happily in these Yale buildings for a while— but it was only for a while. During our residence at the Branford master's house, we knew all the time that *we* were only temporary sojourners there; but the life of the buildings themselves would go on. They might stand for centuries, while a private home lasts for a few generations, if that many, and as time is reckoned is quite a temporary affair. A neighborhood, pleasant today, will most probably change in the course of a few years, the building itself deteriorate, a beloved family residence may during the next generation's tenure be converted into doctors' offices, a funeral parlor, or be razed entirely to provide a parking lot.

But we can count on glorious Harkness Tower to stand firm, unless an act of God or total war destroys everything. As far as can be predicted, the master's house that we (oh, so temporarily) called home, will stand foursquare for hundreds of years to come, and student life, as well as the family life of some master, will go on within its walls. When we left, another family came in, and after them another, and then another, and another and there is a little boy or girl playing in a sandbox today somewhere who will be the master after that. Those who are there today will pass out of the picture, but the feeling of the continuity of family life within these walls is strong.

Even our children were conscious of this. When Prima was in the sixth grade, she showed me a small brass box full of postage stamps that she had planned to hide behind the molding in the closet in her room, and leave there when we moved out. She had enclosed in it a note in her funny little backhand to a future master's daughter: "The time the stamps were placed in this box was May 26, 1946, when I am eleven years old. I am the master's daughter who lives in this room at 80 High Street, New Haven, Connecticut. I have taken them from my collection of stamps and have placed them in this box for the finder's use. Amen." She told me solemnly that she hoped the box would stay hidden for a hundred years, and then another master's daughter, living in that same room, would find them, and the antique stamps would make her fortune.

Anyone's personal life may seem of little account here, but when my husband reached retirement age, and the time had come for us to move out, we felt that by having lived in a master's house, we had become a tiny part of history.

In five hundred years, some graduate student may write an interesting thesis based on my family's commonplace daily routine; some historian, poring over the pages of the little Branford chapel register, come with delight on the then-faded lines that the Yale chaplain wrote so long ago recording a student's marriage, and the christening of the son of some alumnus.

Five hundred years from now, God and the Russians willing, we know that there will still be welcoming fires in the same living room fireplace on winter Sunday afternoons, and students to stretch their long legs before it, and a master's wife to give them tea.